Pontus Hultén during the construction of
She – A Cathedral at Moderna Museet Stockholm in 1966

Pontus Hultén in the exhibition *She – A Cathedral*,
Moderna Museet, 1966

Visitors at the exhibition *She – A Cathedral*,
Moderna Museet, 1966

Pontus Hultén, Andy Warhol and Anna-Lena Wibom
in the Warhol exhibition at Moderna Museet, 1968

Andy Warhol's *Cow* wallpaper on the façade of Moderna Museet, 1968

Pontus Hultén during the installation of the exhibition
The Machine at the Museum of Modern Art, New York, 1968

Pontus Hultén, Claes Oldenburg and
Niki de Saint Phalle at the preview of *The Machine*
at the University of St. Thomas, Houston, 1969

From the exhibition *Utopias and Visions 1871–1981*,
Moderna Museet, 1971

Museum director Pontus Hultén, from the series *Famous Swedes* by the photographer Benno Movin-Hermes, 1971

Pontus Hultén and Moderna Museet.
From Stockholm to Paris

Preface

Gitte Ørskou

Ever since it was first conceived more than sixty years ago, Moderna Museet has been the subject of countless visions, debates, successes and controversies. There have always been strong opinions on what the museum does and doesn't do. Moderna Museet has a legacy of experimenting and venturing outside the expectations of what a modern art museum is. To reflect on this legacy, and to follow in its footsteps or find new pathways, we need knowledge about the Museum's history. Over the past ten years, our research activities have intensified, leading to a number of collaborations with universities and other museums in Sweden and abroad. A bright star among my predecessors was Pontus Hultén, and his career has been the subject of many studies. This book analyses and reconsiders some of the myths about the first decade that still inform the picture of Moderna Museet in many ways. The challenges of leading and running the largest Nordic museum of modern art have obviously changed since Hultén began his work in the early 1960s and laid the foundation for the museum we know. Interestingly, however, many of the issues that Hultén and his colleagues and staff negotiated with regard to the museum of the future are just as relevant now.

Pontus Hultén's own voice resounds in various ways in the project and in this book, through an interview from 1971, in which he responds to the question of how to interest as many people as possible in a museum of contemporary art. He says that we need to have faith in artistic activity as the most subtle yet sharpest form of expression. This statement, which is inspiring in so many ways, is in line with the manifesto we have been developing since 2019, which declares that Moderna Museet shall be engaging, fight for art and be a stimulating place for people and art, in accordance with our assignment to collect, preserve, exhibit and share.

The research project *Pontus Hultén and Moderna Museet – Research and Learning Based on an Art Collection, an Archive and a Library* has been running for many years, and the results have been presented successively as texts, programmes and exhibitions. My warmest thanks go to the project team, which consisted of our internal researchers Annika Gunnarsson, Ylva Hillström and Anna Tellgren, and the external researcher Anna Lundström. Three other researchers were invited to contribute. We would like to thank Patrik Andersson and Jimmy Pettersson for their pieces in the first book, published in 2017, and Lars Bang Larsen for his sharp analysis of *The Machine* in this second book. We are also grateful to Moderna Museet's Archive Manager, Susana Mendoza Brackenhoff, who has supported the projects in its various phases.

The brilliant graphic design of the books was devised by Karl Stefan Andersson. This series on our ongoing research is part of Teresa Hahr's endeavor to develop Moderna Museet's publishing activities in her role as Head of Publications. I also wish to especially thank Walther and Franz König for supporting us and publishing these two books through their legendary publishing house in Cologne, which has been essential for reaching an international readership. Finally, I would like to thank former and current colleagues who have shared their memories and expertise with the researchers, and who will all be inscribed in the history of Moderna Museet.

From the exhibition *Remembering She – A Cathedral*
in the Pontus Hultén Study Gallery, Moderna Museet, 2018

Pontus Hultén and Moderna Museet. Utopias and Visions

Anna Tellgren

The research project *Pontus Hultén and Moderna Museet – Research and Learning Based on an Art Collection, an Archive and a Library* has been in progress since autumn 2015. Over the years, the project has changed and developed and now comprises several different parts.[1] The first part is the book *Pontus Hultén and Moderna Museet. The Formative Years* (2017), which focuses on the period from 1956 to the mid-1960s. It includes a longer introduction, five essays and a previously unpublished text by Pontus Hultén from 1962. The second part of the project is linked to the symposium *Lose Yourself! A Symposium on Labyrinthian Exhibitions as Curatorial Model* held in February 2017 at the Stedelijk Museum in Amsterdam.[2] Based on the exhibitions *Dylaby* (1962) at the Stedelijk and *She – A Cathedral* (1966) at Moderna Museet, it discusses a type of large-scale, collectively created and "labyrinthine" exhibitions. Some of the contributions to the symposium have been edited and published in the web-based magazine *Stedelijk Studies*.[3] The book at hand is the third and final part of this research effort spanning several years, and it deals with a few aspects of Pontus Hultén's later years at Moderna Museet, from the mid-1960s to 1973, when he left Stockholm for Paris. We also take a closer look at some of the projects he worked on after Moderna Museet, which are richly represented in the Pontus Hultén archive.

Alongside producing essays, the project has been mediated in exhibitions and events of various kinds. In the summer of 2018, the exhibition *Remembering She – A Cathedral* was installed in the Pontus Hultén Study Gallery.[4] The exhibition featured the preserved head of the monumental *She* sculpture, together with Hans Hammarskiöld's photographs of the exhibition and a film documentation by Magnus Wibom of the three artists Niki de Saint Phalle, Jean Tinguely and Per Olof Ultvedt building *She* (MOM/2013/148). It also included the model of *She* from 1966, archive material and drawings by the artists. The Study Gallery already had a presentation of material from the archive, films and artworks from the exhibitions *Movement in Art* (1961), *Andy Warhol* (1968), *Ararat. Alternative Research in*

Architecture, Resources, Art and Technology (1976), *Vanishing Points* (1984) and *Implosion. A Postmodern Perspective* (1987). The idea was to give visitors an opportunity to learn more about the museum's history and activities. The material in the Study Gallery has also been activated through guided tours, lectures and seminars.[5] Another collaboration linked to the research project was the master's course "Art and Display" in spring 2019 at Södertörn University, with Moderna Museet, Nationalmuseum and the Museum of Far Eastern Antiquities.[6] Curators from each respective museum held in-depth lectures for the students, who were given access to archives and the Art Library and opportunities to visit the collections. All these activities are in line with the fundamental principle of research at Moderna Museet, which is based on various collaborative projects, focusing on the Museum's exhibitions, history or collection, and utilising its inhouse expertise in curating, conservation, technology and learning.

The field of museum and exhibition studies has expanded and in recent years generated a number of publications and new research projects. How the field had developed since 2008, when we published *The History Book. On Moderna Museet 1958–2008*, was something we had reflected on already when working on our first book in 2017. The series *Exhibition Histories,* published by Afterall Books since 2010, has been significant, with its fundamental theme that exhibitions are key study objects since this is where the audience meets art. From a Nordic perspective, several projects have been initiated to highlight examples of seminal exhibitions and players in Denmark, Finland, Iceland, Norway and Sweden.[7] The interest in the 1960s, with its experimental exhibitions, building the modern art museum and the conditions for art in the post-war era seems to be a strong trend. Several books have recently been published on Pontus Hultén alone and his activities. In connection with its 40th anniversary in 2017, the Centre Pompidou held a panel discussion and published a special edition of *Les Cahiers du Musée national d'art moderne* about Pontus Hultén.[8] The project *Levande arkiv. Pontus Hultén på Moderna Museet och på Centre Pompidou 1957–81* at Södertörn Unviersity has resulted in two publications so far.[9] In 2021, Centre Pompidou-Metz produced the exhibition *Face à Arcimboldo*, with inspiration from Pontus Hultén's exhibition *Effetto Arcimboldo/The Arcimboldo Effect* in 1987 at the Palazzo Grassi in Venice.[10] One of the most recent contributions to the literature on this famous museum director is the book *Pontus Hultén. Den moderna konstens anförare. En biografi* (2022) by the journalist Claes Britton, based on some one hundred interviews, chronicling his life and career to the very end, not merely the legendary formative years that are the focus of many previous studies.

The point of departure for the current project on Pontus Hultén and Moderna Museet has been the ambition to search Moderna Museet's archives, especially Pontus Hulten's own archive (MMA PHA) and the Myndighetsarkivet (the public archive, MMA MA), to highlight topics, events and people that were perhaps not the most visible or obvious. The archives still receive the most requests for documents pertaining to a very small number of early exhibitions, but the Museum's past contains so much more. The work process we have implemented in several of the research projects initiated by the Museum includes both internal and external researchers. This approach expands the museum staff's knowledge and experience with questions and analyses from outside.[11] There is strong criticism against museums and research for focusing excessively on the major male artists, curators and networks. Still, few studies exist on influential female curators in art history.[12] The story of Pontus Hultén, whose early contacts in Paris enabled him to introduce modern art in Stockholm, has been repeated many times over, but the narrative has also been challenged by more recent research that, for instance, identifies the gallery owner Denise René as being a pivotal figure.[13] Swedish exhibition history's strong focus on the major museums and institutions in Stockholm will also change in future research.[14]

In our first book, we noted that one definite result of the five studies on the formative years was that they pointed ahead to another of Pontus Hultén's most famous exhibition, namely the above-mentioned *She – A Cathedral,* shown in summer 1966. In this second book, Ylva Hillström highlights esoteric references in the exhibition and explores it from the perspective of learning. She notes the large number of interpretations of this outstanding project, and the fact that this exhibition is still one of the most renowned in the history of Moderna Museet. Another sign of its popularity is the constant requests to borrow the work *Model for She* from 1966 (MOMSK 266). Exhibitions featuring the model include *Wack! Art and the Feminist Revolution* in 2007 at the Museum of Contemporary Art in Los Angeles, *Niki de Saint Phalle* at Grand Palais in Paris in 2014, *Jean Tinguely. Machine Spectacle* at the Stedelijk Museum in Amsterdam 2016 and one of the latest exhibitions at the Menil Collection in Houston in 2021, *Niki de Saint Phalle in the 1960s*.[15] In line with

From the exhibition *Remembering She – A Cathedral*
in the Pontus Hultén Study Gallery, Moderna Museet, 2018

GRETA GARBO
i
"LUFFAR - PETTER"
"PIERROT-LE-CLOCHARD"
"VAGABUND-PETER"
1922

many of Hultén's exhibition projects, *She – A Cathedral* had an open, audience-friendly, fairground-like side, along with the deeper underlying and more complex elements for those with more knowledge and experience of art history.

Lars Bang Larsen analyses the exhibition *The Machine as Seen at the End of the Mechanical Age*, which Pontus Hultén produced for the Museum of Modern Art (MoMA) in New York, where it opened on 25 November, 1968. This was a prestigious assignment for Hultén, leading to speculation and rumours that he was being considered or had applied for the job as director of MoMA. The exhibition lives on mainly through the brilliantly designed catalogue with a hard metal cover.[16] Lars Bang Larsen highlights a few other projects at the time and draws comparisons with another giant in post-war art, the Swiss curator, artist and art historian Harald Szeemann, and his exhibition *Junggesellenmaschinen/Les Machines célibataires* in 1975 for Kunsthalle Bern. The study ends with a reflection on the exhibition *Mud Muses. A Rant About Technology*, shown at Moderna Museet in 2019, and how the 1960s ideas on art and technology have been handled at the Museum. The rebellious year of 1968 stands out among Moderna Museet's exhibitions in Stockholm and in Pontus Hultén's biography. An exhibition of the American artist Andy Warhol opened already in early spring. This was followed in summer by an exhibition of the Russian artist Vladimir Tatlin, and the autumn show was *The Model. A Model for a Qualitative Society*; nine other exhibitions were presented in the course of the year.

Pontus Hultén's donation to the Museum in 2005 included his library of some 7,000 volumes. In her essay, Annika Gunnarsson reviews and analyses the contents of the library and highlights a few movements and strong sources of inspiration in Hulten's early and subsequent career. Again, Hultén's background and education as a staff member at Nationalmuseum in the 1950s underpins his collecting and his attitude to knowledge. The literature in his library reflects his interest in the new and the artists he was following, but also a more traditional side, with books on general art history and handbooks on art, architecture and film. Several studies have been performed on Hultén's radical way of producing and using exhibition catalogues, and some of his catalogues are collectibles today. Gunnarsson's study clearly reveals how he adopted ideas from Dada, Surrealism, Fluxus and Concrete Poetry, and from people he admired, including Marcel Duchamp and Alfred H. Barr at MoMA.

The concluding essay, by Anna Lundström, is about the art college, or institute of higher art studies, the Institut des Hautes Études en Arts Plastiques (IHEAP) in Paris, which existed from 1988 to 1995. Together with his friends and colleagues Daniel Buren, Serge Fauchereau and Sarkis, Pontus Hultén created a new, radical form of teaching, based mainly on long and initiated discussions between students and guest lecturers. Lundström notes that although this activity was distinctly separate from producing exhibitions, Hultén used the experience, networks and knowledge he had gained through nearly four decades in the service of art.

We are also including an interview with Pontus Hultén from 1971 from the French art magazine *Opus International*, in which he reflects on the museum of the future.[17] It relates to Pontus Hultén's own 1962 essay outlining his ideas on how a modern art museum should be run, which was published in our first book.[18] The text has an introduction by the critic Yann Pavie and is followed by the interview, consisting of ten or so questions on the role and function of the museum in modern society. There is also a short biography on Hultén and an outline of Moderna Museet's history, major exhibitions and acquisitions, and three graphs showing the number of visitors and guided tours from 1958 to 1969. The text is illustrated with a picture of four overlapping circles. This is a model for future activities and different types of information that Moderna Museet was to encompass. The interview was conducted in Paris, where Hultén was in charge of the group exhibition *Alternative Suédoise/Svenskt Alternativ*, a collaboration with Museé d'Art Moderne de la Ville de Paris, which had been shown the year before, in 1970, at Moderna Museet in Stockholm.

After *She – A Cathedral*, eight other exhibitions were produced in autumn 1966, including *Claes Oldenburg. Sculptures and Drawings*, *Young Photographers 1966* and *Peggy Guggenheim's Collection from Venice*. The year after, a retrospective of the Cuban artist Wifredo Lam was featured. Contacts went through Lam's Swedish-born wife, Lou Laurin-Lam.[19] This exhibition was the result of Pontus Hultén's network, and yet another example of how he engaged the Swedish diaspora for his international projects. The engineer Billy Klüver, whom Hultén met when he was still a student, was his most important Swedish contact throughout the rest of his career.[20] Other examples of artists who were presented in solo shows during the second half of Hultén's directorship are Alvar Aalto (1969), Eva Aeppli

From the exhibition *The Model. A Model for a Qualitative Society*, Moderna Museet, 1968

(1968), Vlassis Caniaris (1971), Max Ernst (1969), Lucio Fontana (1967), Bror Hjorth (1967), Piotr Kowalski (1970), Björn Lövin (1971), Meret Oppenheim (1967), Anders Petersen (1970), Paul Thek (1971) and Jean Tinguely (1972).

The exhibition *The Model. A Model for a Qualitative Society* ran for three intense weeks in October 1968. The project has become famous mainly through the fantastic photographic documentation in colour and black-and-white, showing kids of all ages building, playing, painting and jumping around in foam on the floor of the main gallery in Moderna Museet's original building. The visitors to the exhibition included Sweden's then minister of education, Olof Palme, and his sons. This was no finished exhibition; instead, the audience of children created freely in the large wood structure that had been erected. Outside the Museum, more material was available in the form of sand, water, boards and paint. In Moderna Museet's history, *The Model* is often referred to as part of the educational activities and as the origin of the Workshop.[21] The project was in line with the times and was actually a result of a larger discussion on children, pedagogics, learning and schools, and ultimately about how people should live and what their homes should be like, in a modern society. One of the initiators was the Danish artist, architect and teacher Palle Nielsen, who engaged in various activist projects around 1967 to improve urban environments for children. He came in contact with a group in Stockholm that called itself "Aktion Samtal", and their collaboration evolved into the exhibition project *The Model*, which Nielsen subsequently recreated and lectured on in many different contexts.[22] In later years, other members of this collective project have been acknowledged, especially the journalist Gunilla Lundahl, and more nuance has been added to the work process and initiative.[23] *The Model* was clearly one of several examples of alternative, creative activities and environments for children in Stockholm, Copenhagen and other locations. Pontus Hultén wrote a few concluding words in the accompanying publication.[24] According to Lundahl, however, it was Carlo Derkert, senior curator at Moderna Museet at the time, who invited the team to carry out the project. Derkert is described as more open and approachable. According to a report in the archives 33,576 people visited, which can only be regarded as sensational, in view of the short exhibition period.[25] *The Model* was not really followed up in the exhibition programme. There is several examples, however, of another type of thematical exhibitions or projects at the Museum during this period, based on ideas, audience participation, experiments and utopias, and we will return to this further on.

Andy Warhol

One exhibition that is always mentioned in presentations of Moderna Museet and its history is *Andy Warhol*, which opened on 10 February, 1968, and was the artist's first museum exhibition in Europe.[26] The full title was *Andy Warhol Screens, Films, Boxes, Clouds and a Book 1968*, which simply describes the exhibition's contents – an aspect that is somewhat overlooked in the historical narrative.[27] The exhibition lives on in memory for its innovative catalogue and the seven terse posters with a few of Andy Warhol's poignant statements and short quotations in black against a white background. Since then, the Museum has had a close relationship to this artist, and several key works by Warhol were acquired for the collection at an early date. The first was *Marilyn Monroe in Black and White* (1962), featured in the exhibition *American Pop Art. 106 Forms of Love and Despair* (1964) at Moderna Museet and purchased in 1965 from Warhol's gallerist in Paris, Ileana Sonnabend.[28] She attended the preview on 9 February, 1968, in Stockholm, accompanied by her husband, Michael Sonnabend.[29]

In connection with the exhibition *Andy Warhol. Other Voices, Other Rooms* (2008), Olle Granath wrote about his experiences of working on the exhibition forty years earlier, and Kasper König was interviewed.[30] Kasper König had been consulted by the Museum in connection with the Claes Oldenburg exhibition, and he continued to work for the Museum when he was based in New York in 1967 and 1968. There are ten or so handwritten letters from König on thin airmail paper that reveal the process and ideas behind the exhibition and catalogue. For instance, König reported in one of his letters that Warhol wanted to bring the Velvet Underground and asked if Hultén could make a "deal" with Swedish Television.[31] Hultén replied in a letter to Warhol that it would be very expensive for the whole band to come to Stockholm and suggested that he could work with a Swedish band as "stand-in for the 'Velvets'".[32] However, Olle Granath and the secretary Märta Sahlberg handled most of the correspondence with colleagues at other museums, gallery owners, suppliers and the artist. This year was pivotal for Andy Warhol;

Invitation to the *Andy Warhol* exhibition,
Moderna Museet, 1968

on 3 June, 1968, a few months after the exhibition in Stockholm, he was shot by Valerie Solanas, but the Museum's correspondence with Warhol continued for several years due to the touring exhibition and other issues relating to his works.[33] As the director, Pontus Hultén obviously depended on his staff, and he was also planning the exhibition *The Machine* at this time, as mentioned in some of his letters to König.[34]

In recent years, the interest in contacts between Hultén and Warhol has been overshadowed by the Brillo box affair.[35] Facts and memories differ, and the whole matter has been compared to Pontus Hultén's practice of creating replicas of Marcel Duchamp's works, which started with *Movement in Art* (1961), or the building of Tatlin's Tower, formally called *Model for Monument to the Third International* (1919–20), in connection with *Vladimir Tatlin* (1968), yet another exhibition that Pontus Hultén produced in the eventful year of 1968.[36]

A review of the archive material from the Warhol exhibition uncovers a few distinct themes. Financing was a constant worry for the Museum, and there are countless letters from Pontus Hultén and his colleagues asking for financial support and advance funding, and proposals for sharing costs. Another theme is the film *Chelsea Girls* (1966), which was featured in the exhibition in 1968 and was acquired for the Moderna Museet collection (MOMFi 57). One major problem prior to the exhibition opening was getting hold of a copy of the film, and the archive material reveals that the Stockholm end was getting increasingly desperate:

> About *Chelsea Girls*, it is absolutely necessary that it is shown in the exhibition, it is what all people are asking about. … If you have no chance to send it, take it with you.[37]

After the screening in Stockholm, Moderna Museet was inundated with requests from museums, galleries and film clubs all over Europe who wanted to show the film. Some of these were granted, resulting in a tour to 14 venues, including the Filmmuseum in Vienna, the Independent Film Center in Munich, Staatliche Kunstakademie in Düsseldorf, Uppsala Studenters Filmstudio, Cinémathéque Royale de Belgique in Brussels, Odense Bys Museer, Oslo Filmklubb, Norsk Filminstitutt in Oslo and Finlands Filmarkiv in Helsinki.[38] The Museum charged SEK 500 (USD 100) for loans, and it is fascinating to think that this sole copy of a 16 mm film was sent back and forth across Europe – compared to the digital situation today.

There are several letters to and from Andy Warhol's gallery, Leo Castelli in New York. They show that it was far from certain that the two paintings *Ten-Foot-Flowers* (1967) and *Electric Chair* (1967) would remain in Stockholm and the Moderna Museet collection after the exhibition ended.[39] According to Hultén, the agreement with Warhol was that the Museum would fund production of the paintings and that a few works would be left at the Museum. Leo Castelli was not happy at all that Hultén had contacted the artist directly, and neither he nor the artist were aware of having agreed to this.[40] The preserved archive material indicates that there were difficulties getting the works to Stockholm and several copyright issues had emerged. There are also many letters from museums that wanted to feature the exhibition. It eventually toured first to the Stedelijk Museum, Amsterdam, in spring, before half of it went on to Kunsthalle Bern and the other to Kassel, so that Andy Warhol could be presented as part of Documenta 5.[41] The works were then gathered up and shown at Kunstnernes Hus in Oslo in November and December 1968, before the exhibition was dispersed.[42] Plans to include the Institute of Contemporary Arts (ICA) in London and even institutions in Berlin in the tour are mentioned in the correspondence.

Not many people visited the exhibition in Stockholm. The archive mentions 24,633 visitors, and this could be due to the unusually cold weather during the exhibition period, 10 February to 17 March.[43] The catalogue, on the other hand, eventually became a bestseller; several editions were printed and it is now highly sought-after.[44] The correspondence about the catalogue is profuse and includes letters from Gösta Svensson and the company Stig Arbman AB in Malmö, discussing proofs and new editions. There are also letters to booksellers and museums and other contacts, about advance purchases and contributions to cover the cost of printing the catalogue. It was designed by John Melin, a legendary graphic designer and advertising executive, who created Moderna Museet's new graphic profile during Hultén's directorship.[45] The catalogue consists of several introductory quotes by Warhol in English and Swedish, followed by a few hundred black-and-white photographs. The archive contains a letter in which Hultén describes the catalogue texts:

Above: Paul Morrissey, Viva and Andy Warhol at the *Andy Warhol* exhibition, Moderna Museet, 1968. Below: Sonja Martinsson (standing) and unknown staff member at the *Andy Warhol* exhibition, 1968

Above: Andy Warhol, *Photo Album, volumes 1–2*, 1968.
Below: Andy Warhol, spread of *Photo Album, volume 1*, 1968

> The texts at the beginning are going to be only Andy's own statements, we tried to use some of the other texts but the spirit in them is so different that it really broke the unity of the book. With only Andy's statements everything is on the same level which is very important in this case, I think.[46]

The visual material in the catalogue is in three sections. The first documents Andy Warhol's works, photographed by Rudolph Burckhardt, Eric Pollitzer and John D. Schiff. These three photographers seem to have been at the Factory sporadically. The second part is "Factory photos" by Billy Name, and the third is photographs by a young Stephen Shore, also from life in and around the Factory. In a letter, König writes:

> I am working with two good photographers for catalogue. Stephen Shore is very good and is going to print 200–300 prints out of 2,000 for Stockholm. And Billy Linnik [sic!] associate of Factory.[47]

For Stephen Shore, the assignment to photograph at Andy Warhol's Factory was one of his first major jobs. Billy Name was a permanent member of the Factory from 1964, with assignments that included sound and lighting for films and also photography. Among his first images in the catalogue is a series of Pontus Hultén and Billy Klüver and some others visiting Warhol in New York in 1967. They are on a rooftop, testing the buoyancy of an oblong, silver helium balloon. The second and third editions also have a concluding section with photographs of the exhibition installation and the preview at Moderna Museet, taken by the Swedish photographers Nils-Göran Hökby, Bror H. Gustavsson and Peter Gullers. All three had previously worked for Moderna Museet.

The cover shows Warhol's emblematic flowers in pink, orange and lion yellow against a grass-like background in green and black. Different cover ideas were discussed up to the last minute. One of Warhol's ideas was to have a train ticket on the cover and also as a poster design. König asked Hultén to send him a train ticket for Paris–Stockholm or Stockholm–Gothenburg, whatever he deemed suitable.[48] Two air tickets for Andy Warhol with SAS exist, printed on 7 December, 1967, for a trip on 6 January, 1968, to Stockholm, with an open return to New York. These tickets are obviously fake, maculated tickets that someone at the Museum persuaded SAS to print.

Warhol arrived in Stockholm later, just before the exhibition opened. The collection includes a poster in lion yellow of this ticket with black leaves and circles added on top. The work (MOM/2008/12) is a colour silkscreen from 1968 by Stig Arbman AB in Malmö in an edition of 250, which Warhol signed in Stockholm. The catalogue was printed by *Sydsvenska Dagbladet* on thin, lightly-coated newsprint and is reminiscent of a magazine, albeit a bit thicker. It served as part of the exhibition, was sold for SEK 12 (USD 2) and was in keeping with Warhol's ideas on repetition and commercialisation.

A bibliophile edition of the catalogue was also published, on the initiative of Hultén, according to Granath, on account of its popularity.[49] The 100 copies in this second edition from 1969 have gilded book edges and a black acrylic glass case. They were signed by Warhol on his visit to Stockholm in spring 1976. Moderna Museet also has two large photo albums in its photography collection (FM 1968 004 001–002). The two volumes (with more than 500 black-and-white gelatin silver prints) correspond with the contents in the exhibition catalogue, apart from a few prints that are missing. They are mounted on matte black album paper and are in the same order as in the catalogue.[50] The acrylic glass is also used for the protective felt-lined boxes for the black leather albums. Several letters in the archive include data on the catalogue's photographs. They state that they were also used for the press and that a selection was circulated to the institutions that hosted the exhibition.[51] When the tour was over, the photographs were collected and mounted in the two albums, resulting in a unique documentation and object from the exhibition in Stockholm.

Joseph Beuys and Günther Uecker

In the second half of the 1960s, we can discern a few different themes in the Museum's programmes and activities, and in Pontus Hultén's practice. The interest in young American art, which was manifested in exhibitions such as *Four Americans* (1962) and *American Pop Art. 106 Forms of Love and Despair* (1964) subsided after Andy Warhol. This has been interpreted as an attempt to sidestep criticism against the USA in connection with the Vietnam War.[52] The last major show, where Hultén collaborated with his old friend and partner in crime, Billy Klüver, was the exhibition *New York Collection for Stockholm* (1973).[53] In an unpublished manuscript, Hultén wrote the following summary of the first years of activities:

Brillo boxes installed in the *Andy Warhol* exhibition, Moderna Museet, 1968

While I am now, as so many times before, expressing our delight in the Museum's exhibition activities, I must also admit that even this short list suggests a certain deficiency. Deficiency may be too strong a word. Let us call it a lack of balance. I am referring to the fact that modern German art has perhaps not been acknowledged sufficiently and according to merit.[54]

The text was written as a foreword for a catalogue for a double exhibition of the German artists Joseph Beuys and Günther Uecker. But this turned into two solo exhibitions, each with its own catalogue, which were shown simultaneously on 16 January to 28 February, 1971.[55] Hultén pointed out that we could now expect "art to decentralise" and that German art had an important place. The two featured artists were among the best, and they held an absolutely dominant position on the German scene, according to Hultén. The text alludes to difficulties of various kinds in the process, and the fact that there were two separate exhibitions instead of one is probably a result of this. Uecker was not entirely new to the Swedish public, since he had participated in the exhibition *Inner and Outer Space* (1965) with one of his nail pieces.[56] Joseph Beuys, on the other hand, had never before been shown in Sweden. The exhibition presented several objects, including *Hasengrab I–IV* (Hare Grave I–IV), but more importantly drawings from the collection of Franz Joseph and Hans van der Grinten. The Moderna Museet collection contains a collage, *The Daughter of Genghis Khan* (1960), shown in the exhibition and donated by the van der Grinten brothers, who are thanked explicitly by Hultén in the foreword to the catalogue.[57] The exhibition is richly documented, with photographs of Joseph Beuys in his characteristic hat and fur coat working on the Museum premises in Stockholm.

Bernd and Hilla Becher

The year before, in November 1970, Moderna Museet presented an exhibition of the German photographers Bernd and Hilla Becher, titled *Form genom funktion. Fotografisk dokumentation av industribyggnader* (Form Through Function. Photographic Documentation of Industrial Buildings). This was a joint project with the Friends of Fotografiska Museet (FMV). More than 200 black-and-white photographs of the Bechers' typical motifs were featured: gasometers,

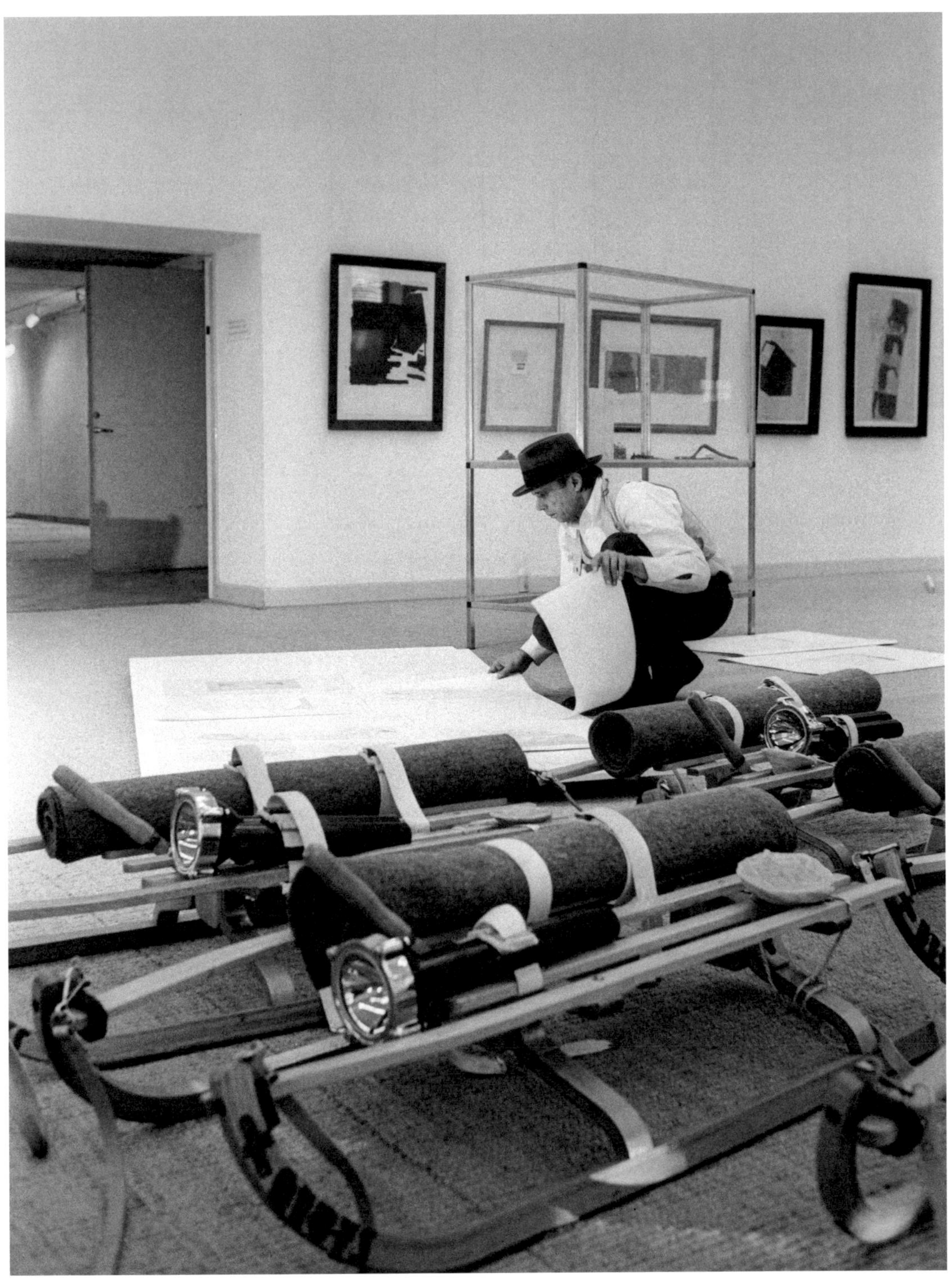

Joseph Beuys at the installation of his exhibition
Actions/Aktionen, Moderna Museet, 1971

Günther Uecker in his nail corner, 1968, from the exhibition catalogue *Günther Uecker. Bildobjekt 1957–1970/ Bild-Objekt 1957–1970*, Moderna Museet, 1971

blast furnaces, mining hoists, cooling towers, lime furnaces, silos and water towers. The exhibition was installed in the upper galleries, where the ceiling was fairly low, and the photographs hung close together, according to the Bechers' type categories. There were also prints arranged on tables and screens standing on the floor. The catalogue is folded and becomes a poster when opened up. An effective design that was used for several other photo exhibitions around that time.[58] In all these exhibition projects with German artists, Karin Bergqvist Lindegren played a prominent part as curator, catalogue editor and translator. We have previously noted that she often stepped in and replaced Hultén when he was travelling or on leave of absence.[59] In a conversation between her, Carlo Derkert, Ingela Lind and Katja Waldén, she describes her way to the Museum.[60] She was an art historian from Lund and began working at Nationalmuseum before getting a permanent position at Moderna Museet in 1961, so she was not one of Hultén's old cronies from university. She was the director of Moderna Museet from 1977 to 1979 – the first and only female director of Moderna Museet until Gitte Ørskou was appointed in 2019.

The Becher show was just one of many photography exhibitions at Moderna Museet in the 1960s and early 1970s. The first was *Svenskarna sedda av 11 fotografer* (Swedes as Seen by 11 Photographers), which opened on 26 December, 1962, and closed on 10 February, 1963.[61] This exhibition featured nearly three hundred black-and-white photographs by a few of Sweden's most established photographers at the time.[62] The exhibition committee consisted of Kurt Bergengren, Stig Claesson, Carlo Derkert and Pontus Hultén, along with the eleven photographers. In spring 1965, *Fotografiska Världsutställningen* (The Photographic World Exhibition) was shown in collaboration with and at Liljevalchs Konsthall. The famous French photographer Édouard Boubat had his first major retrospective abroad in 1967 at Moderna Museet, thanks to his friend and fellow photographer Rune Hassner.[63] Most photography exhibitions at Moderna Museet were then produced in association with the Friends of Fotografiska Museet.[64] The first exhibition organised by the department of photography that was established at Moderna Museet in 1971, known as Fotografiska Museet until the restructuring in 1998, was *André Kertész. Fotografier 1913–1971* (1971).[65] This was the last joint exhibition with the Friends of Fotografiska Museet, but the Friends continued to exist until the end of the 1990s, when it merged with the Friends of Moderna Museet.

From the exhibition *Bernd and Hilla Becher. Form Through Function. Photographic Documentation of Industrial Buildings*, Moderna Museet, 1970

Pontus Hultén was eager to incorporate photography in Moderna Museet's activities, and, according to Olle Granath, this was entirely in line with his ambition that Moderna Museet's collection should cover the same range as the collections of its role model, MoMA in New York.[66]

It is also interesting to note how photographic images were introduced as part of several thematical exhibitions, or as scenography. One facet of this open and broad interest in images is the exhibition *Synligt och osynligt. Vetenskapens nya bilder* (Visible and Invisible. New Images in Science), produced in 1973 for Moderna Museet jointly with Fotografiska Museet.[67] The exhibition was based on a fundamental idea and arranged according to a time scale, a spatial scale and a spectral scale, with photographs of different sizes hung in the first room together with electronic microscopes and other instruments. Pictures of the microcosm (close-ups) and macrocosm (stars and planets) and computer images were also shown. Lennart Nilsson's photographs of human reproduction were presented separately in the Museum's cinema.[68] A basic premise was a belief in the educational potential of images and exhibitions to describe complicated scientific methods and results. Hultén later produced the exhibition *Cartes et figures de la terre* (1980) for Centre Pompidou, about the history of maps.[69] In these projects, Hultén cooperated with the scientific journalists Annagreta and Eric Dyring on their concept and contents.

Utopias and Visions

Moderna Museet's major summer exhibition in 1971 was *Utopias and Visions 1871–1981*, shown outdoors at the old rifle range behind the navy prison on Skeppsholmen. Based on a number of utopian situations, beginning with the Paris Commune in 1871, the exhibition presented material relating to everyday life in this Commune, Buckminster Fuller's World Game, and future communication issues. The exhibition is best remembered for its geodesic dome, where the artist Moki Cherry and the jazz musician Don Cherry presented music, decor, clothes and performances throughout the summer.[70] A few years later, in 1974, Hultén invited them to Paris to create a temporary "Atelier des enfants" prior to the completion of Centre Pompidou.

As an art exhibition, *Utopias and Visions* was both different and typical of the times. Different in that it did not claim to be showing art.

On the contrary, it was a kind of "future research", with advanced technology, audience participation and music as key components. After a historic summary of the Paris Commune, the audience visited a number of stations that all showed different aspects of the world that could materialise already in 1981, if we all chipped in. But this exhibition was also typical of the times. In the early 1970s, Sweden and the West had a politicised social climate. The arts became an arena for (left-wing) political involvement, and art was seen as an instrument for political change. After 1968, Moderna Museet's previously playful, not to say carefree exhibition programme shifted towards a more targeted political agenda. Exhibition such as *Revolutionens språk* (The Language of Revolution) and *Poesin måste göras av alla! Förändra världen!* (Poetry Must be Made by All! Change the World!) (1968–69), visits by the Black Panther Party in 1970, and a book café organised by the socialist bookstore Gamma (1970) are a few of the activities that prompted the parliamentary auditors to describe the Museum's activities as "fiercely agitational" in the report they submitted the same year as *Utopias and Visions* took place.[71] As a whole, the exhibition was also a visionary presentation of what a modern art museum could be. Through its different sections, illustrated on the catalogue cover, a gradual condensation of information and experiences evolves. In the interview published in *OPUS International* the same year, Pontus Hultén describes how the museum could one day serve as a meeting and communication hub, where flows between artists, audiences and society intersect. *Utopias and Visions* can be regarded as an attempt to implement this form of museum.

Another experiment during Pontus Hultén's last years as the director of Moderna Museet was Filialen (The Annex), operated from March 1971 to July 1973, mainly by Pär Stolpe.[72] When Kasern III, the former naval canteen, became available, this gave the Museum more space to work with music, dance, theatre, new visual media, debates, meetings and parties, and to offer yet another forum for its audiences.[73] The activities at Filialen met with criticism and strong opinions and tensions arose between different camps. There were discussions around this time about moving Moderna Museet to Kulturhuset in central Stockholm.[74] The plans for this were engendered by the fundamental concept of the modern art museum that Hultén brought with him and elaborated on during his years at Musée d'art moderne at Centre Pompidou in Paris.[75]

Buckminster Fuller's geodesic dome with Don Cherry performing, at the exhibition *Utopias and Visions 1871–1981*, Moderna Museet, 1971

The museum director Pontus Hultén and his era continue to fascinate, inspire and influence not only the activities today at Moderna Museet, but also art historians, curators and artists internationally. Recent research in exhibition history, which we refer to and apply in this project, has proposed alternative histories and interpretations, and has also highlighted other significant players. In our studies and explorations of particular events in Moderna Museet's early days, some themes stand out, and one of these is the impact of Pontus Hultén's contacts with and educational experiences at Nationalmuseum.[76] What would have happened if Otte Sköld had not died in 1958, only a year after becoming the director of Moderna Museet? Much of what the young Pontus Hultén implemented already existed as ideas and discussions on the mother ship, Nationalmuseum, but we can also confirm that Hultén, with his interests and early travels, was well-prepared and saw the potential. He was simply the right man in the right place at the right time. He also had a remarkable ability to attract talented and loyal staff members, as a deep look into the archives and the interviews with some of his old friends and colleagues will reveal. Another theme is how Pontus Hultén intentionally built and employed networks throughout his career. Collaborations with his Nordic colleagues at Louisiana Museum of Modern Art in Humlebæk outside Copenhagen and Henie Onstad Kunstsenter at Høvikodden outside Oslo are particularly interesting, along with the other museums and art institutions of the same size as Moderna Museet in its early days.[77] The visions of the modern art museum formulated in the 1960s resound in public debate to this day, but the conditions have, of course, changed. Knowledge and analysis of history gives us the potential to relate to and pass on the legacy of this era to the future. This book follows Pontus Hultén and his activities from his hometown, Stockholm, via New York, and back to his second hometown, Paris.

1. For more on the research project, Pontus Hultén's donation in 2005, the collection, the archive, the library and the Study Gallery, and for a biography of Pontus Hultén (1924–2006), see Anna Tellgren, "Pontus Hultén and Moderna Museet. Research and learning based on an art collection, an archive and a library", *Pontus Hultén and Moderna Museet. The Formative Years,* eds. Anna Tellgren and Anna Lundström, Stockholm: Moderna Museet and London: Koenig Books, 2017, pp. 15–35. The project was financed for two years (2015–16) by the Swedish Arts Council's funding for research at Central Museums.

2. The symposium was on 2–4 February, 2017, and was co-organised by Moderna Museet in Stockholm, Museum Tinguely in Basel, the Stedelijk Museum and the Dutch Postgraduate School for Art History (OSK) Vrije Universitet in Amsterdam. The organisational team included Angela Bartholomew, Dorine de Bruijne, Annika Gunnarsson, Ylva Hillström, Katja Kwastek, Anna Lundström, Andres Pardey, Margriet Schavemaker and Anna Tellgren.

3. See "Lose Yourself! On Labyrinthine Exhibitions as Curatorial Model", *Stedelijk Studies*, issue no. 7, 2018. https://stedelijkstudies.com/journal-archive/issue-7-lose-yourself/ (23 August, 2022).

4. The exhibition ran from 3 June, 2018 to 3 February, 2019. It was curated by Anna Tellgren. See https://www.modernamuseet.se/stockholm/sv/utstallningar/att-minnas-hon-en-katedral/ (23 August, 2022).

5. The research project was communicated to the public through three lectures at the Tuesday Club (8 November, 2016, 21 November, 2017, and 23 October, 2018), organised by the Friends of Moderna Museet (MMV). See also Anna Tellgren, "Forskning pågår Pontus Hultén & Moderna Museet", *Bulletinen Moderna Museets Vänner*, no. 2, 2016, p. 15, and Annika Gunnarsson, "Fest, fantastiskt och forskning", *Bulletinen Moderna Museets Vänner*, no. 3, 2017, p. 18. The seminar series *Om utställningar* (On Exhibitions) took place on three occasions in 2017: on *Dylaby* and *Hon* (10 February), a conversation between Olle Granath, Jens Hoffmann and Maria Lind (11 April), and on *Implosion* with Lars Nittve interviewed by Lars Bang Larsen (21 November). The series of talks *Sex till åtta* (Six to Eight) was held in conjunction with the exhibition *Warhol 1968* on three occasions in autumn 2018 and was co-organised with Södertörn University.

6. The course "Exponeringens effekter: Utställningsmediets formering i 1960-talets nationella museer" (1011KV) was held at second-cycle and postgraduate level (7.5 credits) and was co-organised by Södertörn University, Moderna Museet, Nationalmuseum and the Museum of Far Eastern Antiquities. It was planned by Annika Öhrner, associate professor and senior lecturer in art history at Södertörn University, together with the curator Anna Tellgren, head of research at Moderna Museet.

7. See Anne Gregersen, Kristian Handberg and Michael Kjær, "Udstillingen som forskningsobjekt. Skandinaviske Exhibition Histories", *Periskop. Forum for kunsthistorisk debat*, no. 20, 2018, pp. 5–11. Another example of this from a Nordic perspective is the art historian conference NORDIK XII

(organised by the Nordic Association for Art Historians) in Copenhagen in autumn 2018, with two sessions on exhibition history: *Remembering – Art History and Curatorial Practices in Nordic Post-War Exhibition Studies* (led by Anna Lundström and Anna Tellgren) and *Futures from the Past? Nordic Exhibition Histories* (led by Anne Gregersen, Kristian Handberg and Michael Kjær).

8. *Hommage à Pontus Hultén* was organised at Centre Pompidou in Paris on 24 November, 2017. The panel consisted of Daniel Birnbaum, Bernard Blistène, Daniel Buren and Serge Fauchereau. The special issue of *Les Cahiers du Musée national d'art moderne*, Paris: Éditions du Centre George Pompidou, no. 141, autumn 2017, was followed by a special issue on the exhibition *Paris–Moscou 1900–1930* (1979), one of the so-called city exhibitions that Pontus Hultén produced at Centre Pompidou: *"Paris–Moscou" 40 ans après, Les Cahiers du Musée national d'art moderne,* Paris: Éditions du Centre George Pompidou, hors-série 2019.

9. The project team consisted of Charlotte Bydler, Andreas Gedin and Sinziana Ravini. The publications published within the project are: Andreas Gedin, *Pontus Hultén, She, a Cathedral & Moderna Museet*, London: Koenig Books, 2020, and *Pontus Hultén på Moderna Museet. Vittnesseminarium, Södertörns högskola, 26 april 2017*, eds. Charlotte Bydler, Andreas Gedin and Johanna Ringarp, Samtidshistoriska frågor 38, Huddinge: Södertörn University, 2018.

10. See Anne Horvath, "L'effet Pontus Hultén", *Face à Arcimboldo* (exh. cat.), eds. Chiara Parisi and Anne Horvath, Metz: Èdition du Centre Pompidou-Metz, 2021, pp. 385–391.

11. See also *Forskning vid museer,* ed. Fredrik Svanberg, The Museum of National Antiquities, Stockholm Studies 19, Stockholm: Historiska Museet and Stockholm: Swedish Arts Council, 2011.

12. Hans Ulrich Obrist includes two women, Anne d'Harnoncourt and Lucy Lippard, among the eleven curators he interviewed and mentions in his book *A Brief History of Curating*, Zürich: JRP Ringier, 2008. See also *From Conceptualism to Feminism. Lucy Lippard's Numbers Shows 1969–74,* Exhibition Histories, London: Afterall Books and London: Koenig Books, 2012.

13. See also Marta Edling, "From Margin to Margin? The Stockholm Paris Axis 1944–1953", *Konsthistorisk tidskrift/Journal of Art History*, vol. 88, no. 1, 2019, pp. 1–16.

14. See, for instance, Katarina Wadstein MacLeod, *From Flux to Festivity. Iternational Art in Lunds konsthall 1965–67*, eds. Elin Aspeklev, Anders Kreuger, Åsa Nackning and Emil Nilsson, Södertörn Studies in Art History and Aesthetics 6, Lund: Lunds konsthall and Huddinge: Södertörn University, 2022.

15. More than 20 loan requests have been granted since 2000, and the work has travelled to several major art museums in Europe and the USA, in addition to being shown for long periods in the collection at Moderna Museet in Stockholm (2004 and 2007) and in the exhibition *Niki de Saint Phalle. The Girl, the Monster and the Goddess* at Moderna Museet Malmö

in 2012 and in Stockholm in 2013, and in the Pontus Hultén Study Gallery in 2018. See the catalogues: *Wack! Art and the Feminist Revolution* (exh. cat.), ed. Lisa Gabrielle Mark, Los Angeles: The Museum of Contemporary Art, 2007, p. 180; *Niki de Saint Phalle 1930–2002* (exh. cat.), ed. Camille Morineau, Paris: Réunion des musées nationaux – Grand Palais, 2014, p. 85; *Jean Tinguely*, Stedelijk Museum Amsterdam catalog number 927, eds. Margriet Schavemaker, Barbara Til and Beat Wismer, Amsterdam: Stedelijk Museum and Cologne: Verlag der Buchhandlung Walther König, 2016, p. 136; *Niki de Saint Phalle in the 1960s* (exh. cat.), eds. Jill Dawsey and Michelle White, Houston: The Menil Collection and San Diego: Museum of Contemporary Art, 2021, p. 186.

16. *The Machine as Seen at the End of the Mechanical Age* (exh. cat.), ed. K. G. Pontus Hultén, New York: The Museum of Modern Art, 1968. There is plenty of archive material on the catalogue for *The Machine*, which was produced by the same group (Pontus Hultén, John Melin and Gösta Svensson) that made the famous catalogue for the Andy Warhol exhibition the same year. See note 44. The cover for *The Machine* was designed by Anders Österlin, one half of the Melin & Österlin duo. See Utställningar, 68 The Machine. MMA PHA 4.2.52–58.

17. Yann Pavie, "Vers le musée du futur. Entretien avec Pontus Hultén", *Opus International*, no. 24–25, 1971, pp. 56–65. A copy of the article is found in the material about Filialen. MMA MA F1a:57. See also Yann Pavie, "Entretien avec H. Szeemann", *Opus International*, no. 36, 1972, pp. 38–44.

18. Pontus Hultén, "How Does One Wish a Museum for Modern Art to Function?", *Pontus Hultén and Moderna Museet. The Formative Years*, 2017, pp. 177–181. The text is attached to a letter to Professor Pieter Sanders dated 4 December, 1962. MMA PHA 4.1.52.

19. The exhibition documents include approximately 10 letters from Lou Laurin-Lam, discussing the exhibition and texts for the catalogue. MMA MA F1a:38. See also *Wifredo Lam. Hjärtats snår, vapen, frukter*, eds. K.G. Hultén and Barbro Sylwan, Moderna Museet exhibition catalogue no. 62, Stockholm: Moderna Museet, 1967.

20. Pontus Hultén, "The New York Connection", *Moderna Museet 1958–1983*, eds. Olle Granath and Monica Nieckels, Stockholm: Moderna Museet, 1983, pp. 54–57, and Marianne Hultman, "Our Man in New York. An Interview with Billy Klüver on His Collaboration with Moderna Museet", *The History Book. On Moderna Museet 1958–2008*, eds. Anna Tellgren and Martin Sundberg, Stockholm: Moderna Museet and Göttingen: Steidl, 2008, pp. 233–256.

21. See Birgitta Arvas, "Barn på Moderna Museet – VERKSTAN", *Moderna Museet 1958–1983*, 1983, pp. 187–195, and Anette Göthlund, "Activities in the Workshop and Zon. Art Education for Children at Moderna Museet", *The History Book. On Moderna Museet 1958–2008*, 2008, pp. 257–296.

22. Lars Bang Larsen, *Palle Nielsen. The Model. A Model for a Qualitative Society* (1968), Barcelona: Museu d'Art Contemporani de Barcelona (MACBA), 2010. The book was published in conjunction with Palle Nielsen's

donation of his archive to MACBA in 2009, with drawings, photographs, LPs and other material from *The Model*. See also Palle Nielsen, "A Brief History of the Model", *The Model Palle Nielsen* (exh. cat.), eds. Christian Gether, Stine Høholt, Dorthe Juul Rugaard and Camilla Jalving, Ishøj: Arken Museum of Modern Art, 2015, pp. 68–71.

23. Gunilla Lundahl, "The Model, Action Dialogue and a Conversation over Time", *The New Model: An Inquiry. Tensta konsthall*, eds. Maria Lind and Lars Bang Larsen, Berlin: Sternberg Press, 2020, pp. 31–40. See also Lars Bang Larsen and Maria Lind in the same publication, "Interview with Gunilla Lundahl. Tensta konsthall, November 8, 2017", *The New Model: An Inquiry*, 2020, pp. 111–132. After *The Model* closed at Moderna Museet, the entire exhibition was moved to the new housing district Råby in Västerås, where it was renamed *Ballongen* (The Balloon). For more information, see *Den fria leken. Modellen, Ballongen och konsten som action*, ed. Katrin Ingelstedt, Stockholm: Folkrörelsernas konstfrämjande and Västerås: Västerås konstmuseum, 2017.

24. K. G. P. Hultén, "Museernas nya roll", *Modellen. En modell för ett kvalitativt samhälle*, Stockholm: Moderna Museet, 1968, p. 32. This thin pamphlet contains short quotes and texts from: Arbetsgruppen (the exhibition team), Mats G. Bengtsson, Clas Engström, Sigmund Freud, André Gorz, John Holt, Sören Kierkegaard, R. D. Laing, Sven Lindner, Gunilla Lundahl, Hjördis Nilsson, Palle Nielsen, Leif Nylén, Mette Prawitz, Ludvig Rasmusson, Iréne and Bengt Sjöblom, Bertil Söderling, Anna-Clara Tjerneld (Tidholm), Jan Thomæus, Kerstin and Olle Wickman, Tomas Wieslander, Mao Zedong, Per-Johan Ödman, a few anonymous children, Vasastans byalag and the headmaster's office in Norra Ängby.

25. Visitors: Paying adults (8,975), Groups (8,726), Children with parents (10,875), Others (5,000). *The Model*, 30 September–23 October, 1968. Breakdown as of 31 October, 1968. MMA MA F1a:46.

26. On the 50th anniversary, the exhibition *Warhol 1968* opened at Moderna Museet in Stockholm in autumn 2018, and in spring 2019 at Moderna Museet Malmö. The curator was John Peter Nilsson. See also John Peter Nilsson, "Warhol 1968", *Moderna Museets Vänner* no. 3, 2018, pp. 4–5. The exhibition mainly featured works from the collection (there are around hundred works by Andy Warhol) and a few of the *Cow* wallpaper panels that were shown in 1968 had been brought out from storage and conserved. See more about the wallpaper at https://www.modernamuseet.se/stockholm/sv/2019/04/18/bakom-kulisserna-andy-warhols-cow-wallpaper (23 August, 2022). The archive contains a proposal by Gösta Wibom on how the wallpaper should be mounted, 2 January, 1967. MMA MA F1a:42.

27. See the small invitation card to the preview on 10 February, 1968, with the same flower as the catalogue cover. MMA MA B5:2. The exhibition was on until 17 March.

28. Annika Öhrner, "On the Construction of Pop Art. When American Pop Arrived in Stockholm in 1964", *Art in Transfer in the Era of Pop. Curatorial Practices and Transnational Strategies*, ed. Annika Öhrner, Södertörn Studies in Art History and Aesthetics 3, Huddinge: Södertörn University,

2017, pp. 127–159. See also Annika Öhrner, "Warhol in Translation, Stockholm 1968: 'Many Works and Few Motifs'", *Journal of Art Historiography*, no. 26, June 2022. https://arthistoriography.wordpress.com/26-jun22/ (23 August, 2022).

29. Thank-you letter from Ileana Sonnabend to K.G. Hultén, 27 February, 1968. MMA MA F1a:41.

30. Olle Granath, "With Andy Warhol 1968", *Andy Warhol. A Guide to 706 Objects in 2 Hours 56 Minutes, Other Voices, Other Rooms,* ed. Eva Meyer-Hermann, Moderna Museet exhibition catalogue no. 343, Stockholm: Moderna Museet and Rotterdam: NAi Publishers, 2008, 00.10–00.13. He also said at the witness seminar at Södertörn University on 26 April, 2017 that he served as "some kind of executive at the Warhol exhibition", and that he was not paid for this. See *Pontus Hultén på Moderna Museet*, 2018, p. 57. The financial records list various expenses and travel funding for Olle Granath. Expenses–Warhol. MMA MA F1a:42.

31. Letter from Kasper König to Pontus Hultén, undated 1967. MMA MA F1a:41.

32. Letter from unknown, probably Pontus Hultén, to Andy Warhol, 8 January, 1968. MMA MA F1a:41. The letter states that the leader of the Swedish band, Thomas Tidholm, will be sending a separate letter. The band, Pärsons Sound, which later became Träd, Gräs och Stenar, played once during the exhibition. This is documented in the final picture in the second and third editions of the catalogue. See *Andy Warhol*, eds. Andy Warhol, Kasper König, Pontus Hultén and Olle Granath, Stockholm: Moderna Museet and Malmö: Stig Arbman AB, 1970.

33. The secretary Märta Sahlberg writes to Warhol in July apologising for disturbing him on account of the incident. Letter from Märta Sahlberg to Andy Warhol, 26 July, 1968. MMA MA F1a:41.

34. Letter from Pontus Hultén to Kasper König, 3 May, 1968. MMA MA F1a:41.

35. Pontus Hultén ordered 125 wooden Brillo boxes to be made for several exhibitions in the 1990s. There is an undated note in the archives, "P.M. Concerning Brillo Boxes" by Pontus Hultén. Exhibitions, 1953–1977. MMA PHA 4.2.17. This is the text that was published in *Pontus Hultén's Collection*, ed. Iris Müller-Westermann, Moderna Museet exhibition catalogue no. 321, Stockholm: Moderna Museet, 2004, p. 360. See "Second Report: The Stockholm Type Boxes Prepared by the Andy Warhol Art Authentication Board", 19 July, 2010, Reg. no. MM 2010-183-254. MMA MA F2eb:12. See also Thomas Anderberg, *Den stora konstsvindeln*, Stockholm: Bokförlaget Atlas, 2010.

36. See Paul B. Franklin, "Exposing Duchamp in Sweden", *Étant donné Marcel Duchamp,* no. 11, ed. Paul B. Franklin, Paris: Association pour l'Étude de Marcel Duchamp, 2016, pp. 94–141. Nathalie Leleu, "'Let Us Place the Eye Under the Control of Touch.' Replicas and Replicators of Vladimir Tatlin's Monument to the Third International: The Great Adventure of Pontus Hulten", *Tatlin: New Art for a New World*, Basel: Museum Tinguely

and Ostfildern: Hatje Cantz, 2012, pp. 122–129. See also Ulf Linde and Per Olof Ultvedt, "Rapport om rekonstruktionen", *Vladimir Tatlin*, eds. Karin Bergqvist Lindegren, K. G. P. Hultén and Douglas Feuk, Moderna Museet exhibition catalogue no. 75, Stockholm: Moderna Museet, 1968, pp. 26–27.

37. Letter from unknown, probably Pontus Hultén, to Andy Warhol, 8 January, 1968. MMA MA F1a:41.

38. See the correspondence in the archive (MMA MA F1a:41–42) on the screenings of Moderna Museet's copy of *Chelsea Girls*, compiled by David Nasri, intern at the Museum in spring 2018.

39. They were deposited at the Museum from 1968 until 1976, when the acquisitions were finalised. *Ten-Foot-Flowers* (MOM 57) was donated by the artist, and *Electric Chair* (MOM 58) was donated by Kasper König.

40. Letters from Leo Castelli to Pontus Hultén 21 May, 1970 and 15 June, 1970. MMA MA F1a:42.

41. Letter from Harald Szeemann to Pontus Hultén, 8 May, 1968. MMA MA F1a:41.

42. Letter from the curator Thomas Mürer to Pontus Hultén, 21 August, 1967. MMA MA F1a:41.

43. Visitors to the Warhol exhibition, 10 February–17 March, 1968: 24,633, of which 7,519 in the evening. MMA MA F1a:42. The exhibition had fewer visitors than *The Model*, which was shown for around two weeks less.

44. *Andy Warhol,* eds. Andy Warhol, Kasper König, Pontus Hultén and Olle Granath, Stockholm: Moderna Museet, and Malmö: Stig Arbman AB, 1968. Second edition 1969 and third edition 1970. In a letter shortly after the opening, Pontus Hultén asks Kasper König to give away a few copies of the catalogue to "influential people", because it is not selling that well. Letter from Pontus Hultén to Kasper König, 18 February, 1968. MMA MA F1a:41. Regarding the catalogue, see "Willem de Roij on Andy Warhol", *Other Voices, Other Rooms*, 2008, pp. 02.30–02.31.

45. See *John Melin till exempel. En hyllning till det enkla, vackra, lekfulla, konstnärliga, unika, egensinniga, tidlösa, moderna, experimentella*, ed. Johan Melbi, Stockholm: Moderna Museet, 1999.

46. Letter from Pontus Hultén to Kasper König, 20 December, 1967. MMA MA F1a:41. Olle Granath was the one who compiled the texts based on articles and interviews with Andy Warhol. He says that it was Pontus Hultén who coined one of Warhol's most famous quotes: "In the future everybody will be world famous for fifteen minutes". Olle Granath, *Other Voices, Other Rooms*, 2008, p. 00.13.

47. Letter from Kasper König to Pontus Hultén, undated 1967. MMA MA F1a:41. Billy Name's original name was William George Linich.

48. Letter from Kasper König to Pontus Hultén, 1 December, 1967. MMA MA F1a:41. *Photo Album Volume 1* (FM 1968 004 001) includes two copies of Andy Warhol's fake SAS air ticket, glued in.

49. Olle Granath, *Other Voices, Other Rooms*, 2008, p. 00.13. See also a letter from Gösta Svensson to Olle Granath, 27 May, 1968, concerning a possible special binding of the Warhol book. MMA MA F1a:42.

50. The photographs where probably collected and pasted into the albums at Stig Arbman AB in Malmö, where the catalogue was printed. This theory is confirmed by Leif Wigh, curator of photography at Moderna Museet between 1973 and 2004, in an e-mail to Anna Tellgren, 25 August, 2022. Olle Granath was also asked, and he thinks that the albums adhere to John Melin's idea, but he has no detailed memory from when they were ordered or by whom. Conversation with Anna Tellgren, 5 May, 2022.

51. Letter from the press officer Sonja Martinsson to A. J. Petersen, Stedelijk Museum, 20 March, 1968. MMA MA F1a:41. The Museum sent 20 original photographs by Billy Name and 20 by Stephen Shore to Amsterdam, stating that it was very important that they were returned when the exhibition ended.

52. Patrik Andersson, *Euro-Pop. The Mechanical Bride Stripped Bare in Stockholm* (diss.), Vancouver: University of British Columbia, 2001.

53. Marianne Hultman, "New York Collection for Stockholm", *Teknologi för livet. Om Experiments in Art and Technology*, Paris: Schultz Förlag AB and Norrköping: Norrköpings Konstmuseum, 2004, pp. 160–171. *New York Collection for Stockholm*, ed. Björn Springfeldt, Moderna Museet exhibition catalogue no. 111, Stockholm: Moderna Museet, 1973.

54. Manuscript by Pontus Hultén 1971. MMA MA F1:59.

55. *Joseph Beuys. Aktioner/Aktionen. Teckningar och objekt 1937–1970 ur samling van der Grinten*, ed. Karin Bergqvist Lindegren, Moderna Museet exhibition catalogue no. 90, Stockholm: Moderna Museet, 1971. *Günther Uecker. Bildobjekt 1957–1970/Bild-Objekt 1957–1970*, ed. Karin Bergqvist Lindegren, Moderna Museet exhibition catalogue no. 91, Stockholm: Moderna Museet, 1971.

56. Patrik Andersson, "Inner and Outer Space. Rethinking Movement in Art", *Pontus Hultén and Moderna Museet. The Formative Years*, 2017, pp. 39–63.

57. The collection also includes the sculpture *Hasengrab V (die Alpen)* (1965) (NMSK 2096), donated to the Museum in 1971 by the Friends of Moderna Museet. For more on the exhibition, see Simone Schmid, *Beuys und Lothar Wolleh. Das Underwasserbuch-Projekt/Wolleh: Beuys. Från Moderna Museet till Undervattenbokprojektet*, Stockholm: Goethe-Institut Schweden, 2021.

58. The same poster format was used for: *Lucien Clergue. Fotografier 1954–1967*, ed. Douglas Kneedler, Moderna Museet exhibition catalogue no. 79, Stockholm: Moderna Museet and Stockholm: Fotografiska Museets Vänner, 1969; *Bernhard and Hilla Becher. Form genom funktion. Fotografisk dokumentation av industribyggnader,* ed. Karin Bergqvist Lindegren, Moderna Museet exhibition catalogue no. 88, Stockholm: Moderna Museet and Stockholm: Fotografiska Museets Vänner, 1970; *Folket och maktens murar. Bilder av Gun Kessle. Text av Jan Myrdal*, ed. Åke Sidwall, Moderna Museet exhibition catalogue no. 95, Stockholm: Moderna Museet and Stockholm: Fotografiska Museets Vänner, 1971; *Fotografisk Vårutställning*, eds. Ulla

Bergman, Åke Sidwall and Leif Wigh, Moderna Museet exhibition catalogue no. 148, Stockholm: Moderna Museet and Stockholm: Fotografiska Museet, 1977.

59. Annika Gunnarsson, "Sam Francis and Claes Oldenburg. Two Americans", *Pontus Hultén and Moderna Museet. The Formative Years,* 2017, p. 137.

60. Ingela Lind, "Vägarna till Moderna Museet", *Moderna Museet 1958–1983,* 1983, pp. 151–158. While working on *The History Book* (2008), Martin Sundberg contacted Karin Bergqvist Lindegren on several occasions to request an interview, but she declined.

61. See Anna Tellgren, "Carlo Derkert och Svenskarna sedda av 11 fotografer", *Biblis,* no. 57, 2012, pp. 49–52. *Svenskarna sedda av elva fotografer*, eds. Carlo Derkert and Pontus Hultén, Moderna Museet exhibition catalogue no. 25, Stockholm: Moderna Museet, 1962.

62. The following photographers participated in the exhibition: Sten Didrik Bellander, Jan Delden, Hans Hammarskiöld, Sune Jonsson, Tore Johnson, Stig T. Karlsson, Lennart Nilsson, Pål-Nils Nilsson, Lennart Olson, Lennart af Petersens and Rolf Winquist.

63. Rune Hassner, "Ögonblick av lycka", *Édouard Boubat* (exh. cat.), ed. Sonja Martinsson, Stockholm: Fotografiska Museet, 1967, unpaginated. See also Rune Hassner, *Bilder & Ord. Bibliografi, filmografi, utställningsförteckning, med mera*, eds. Rune Hassner and Birgitta Forsell, Visuellt Konst- och bildvetenskapliga institutionens skriftserie no. 7, Gothenburg: University of Gothenburg, 2002.

64. The society was formed in 1963 in conjunction with the work on *Svenskarna sedda av 11 fotografer.* Se Pär Frank, "Fotografiska Museet och dess vänner", *Fotografica 67,* Årsskrift för Fotografiska Museets Vänner, Stockholm: Albert Bonniers Förlag, 1966, pp. 83–89.

65. On Fotografiska Museet in Moderna Museet, see Anna Tellgren, "Photography and Art. On The Moderna Museet Collection of Photography from a Historic Perspective on the Institution", *The History Book. On Moderna Museet 1958–2008,* 2008, pp. 121–152.

66. Interview with Olle Granath, 13 June, 2007. See also Olle Granath, "Pontus Hultén à Stockholm", *Les Cahiers du Musée national d'art moderne,* no. 141, 2017, pp. 31–45.

67. *Synligt och osynligt. Vetenskapens nya bilder*, eds. Annagreta Dyring and Eric Dyring, Moderna Museet exhibition catalogue no. 108, Stockholm: Moderna Museet and Stockholm: Allmänna Förlaget, 1973.

68. Pontus Hultén had proposed an exhibition with the photographer Lennart Nilsson early on, but this multifaceted exhibition with images from natural sciences, technology and medicine was organised instead. Minutes from the FMV board meeting 30 September, 1971. MMA FMA A1:3. See also Solveig Jülich, "Lennart Nilsson's Fish-Eyes: A Photographic and Cultural History of Views from Below", *Konsthistorisk tidskrift/Journal of Art History*, vol. 84, no. 2, 2015, pp. 75–92.

69. On the exhibition concepts, see also Annagreta Dyring "Fotot hör hemma i stora sammanhang", *Moderna Museet 1958–1983,* 1983, pp. 166–168.

70. In connection with the exhibition *Moment – Moki Cherry* (9 April, 2016–9 April, 2017) at Moderna Museet in Stockholm, Anna Lundström presented material on *Utopias and Visions 1871–1981* from the archives in a showcase together with a text. MMA MA F1:60 and MMA PHA 4.2.51. The following discussion is based on this presentation.

71. PM on an inspection, no. 8/1971. Further correspondence 1964–1973. MMA MA E5:5. For more on the increasingly political exhibitions at Moderna Museet and MoMA in the 1970s, see Mary Anne Staniszewski, "Looking for Signs of Life", *Konsthistorisk tidskrift/Journal of Art History*, vol. 78, no. 4, 2009, pp. 193–203.

72. Pär Stolpe, *Filialen vid Moderna Museet i Stockholm 1.3 1971–1.7 1973 Rapporten*, Stockholm: Moderna Museet, 1974. MMA MA B7D:1. The report states that Pär Stolpe was responsible for activities at Filialen, with the assistance of Karin Lutturp and Susanne Törneman.

73. Karin Malmquist, "La Cour des miracles. On Visitors, Learning and Art at Moderna Museet", *The History Book. On Moderna Museet 1958–2008*, 2008, pp. 281–296.

74. An early presentation of the plans to move Moderna Museet to Sergels torg is given in an article by Bo Andersson, Carlo Derkert, Pontus Hultén, Li Lind, Pär Stolpe and Anna-Lena Thorsell, "Ett kulturhusprogram: Experiment i social samverkan", *Dagens Nyheter*, 9 September, 1969. See also Kim West, *The Exhibitionary Complex. Exhibition, Apparatus, and Media from Kulturhuset to the Centre Pompidou, 1963–1977* (diss.), Södertörn Studies in Art History and Aesthetics 4, Huddinge: Södertörn University, 2017.

75. Benadette Dufrêne, "La muséologie selon Pontus Hulten", *Les Cahiers du Musée national d'art moderne,* no. 141, 2017, pp. 59–77. See also *Centre Pompidou, trente ans d'histoire*, ed. Bernadette Dufrêne, Paris: Éditions du Centre Pompidou, 2007.

76. Jimmy Pettersson, *Film på konstmuseum. Nationalmuseums möten med filmmediet 1945–1950* (diss.), Stockholm: Stockholm University, 2019.

77. On Pontus Hultén after Moderna Museet, see Claes Britton, *Pontus Hultén. Den moderna konstens anförare. En biografi*, Stockholm: Albert Bonnier Förlag, 2022, pp. 347–749. On Moderna Museet after Pontus Hultén, see Tintin Hodén, *Motsättningarnas museum. Samproduktionen av museiideal i den offentliga debatten om Moderna Museet 1972–2013* (diss.), Linköping Studies in Arts and Sciences no. 791, Linköping: Linköping University. See also the symposium *Utopias and Visions. On the Legacy of Pontus Hultén and His Time*, 18 November, 2022 at Moderna Museet. https://www.modernamuseet.se/stockholm/en/event/utopier-och-visioner-om-arvet-efter-pontus-hulten/ (27 March, 2023).

SHE –
A CATHEDRAL

Niki de Saint Phalle during the construction of
She – A Cathedral, Moderna Museet, 1966

She – A Cathedral. Esoteric Themes and Mediation

Ylva Hillström

The exhibition *She – A Cathedral* (1966) has been interpreted in many different ways over the years. It has been analysed from a gender perspective, as a response to 1960s arts policy objectives, as an example of ground-breaking exhibition practices, as a satire on society and museum institutions, and as a facet of mediaeval carnival culture.[1] In this essay, the focus is on an aspect of the exhibition that has remained relatively unexplored until now, namely its roots in myth and religion. Special attention is given to references to esoteric currents, both in the exhibition itself and in the material relating to its creation. Finally, the capacity of the audience to embrace the many layers of the exhibition is discussed.

She – A Cathedral opened on 4 June, 1966, and was the result of intense collaboration between Jean Tinguely, Niki de Saint Phalle and Per-Olof Ultvedt. *She* was a gigantic sculpture – 23.5 metres long, 6 metres high and 10 metres wide – of a reclining pregnant woman. The entrance between her legs led to a labyrinthine interior. A mini-cinema inside *She* showed a scene from the silent movie *Luffar-Petter* (Peter the Tramp) from 1921, starring Greta Garbo. A bar with a vending machine was installed in one of her breasts. There were plans for a planetarium with illuminated ping-pong balls representing the Milky Way, but it is uncertain whether it was ever actually built.[2] In one of the thighs was a miniature exhibition of paintings that looked as though they had been made by artists such as Paul Klee, Jean Dubuffet or Jean Fautrier but were in fact "fakes" by art critic and musician Ulf Linde.[3] The interior also had room for a slide for kids, stairs, a lovers' seat, a bottle-crushing machine, a phone booth, live fish in a small pond, a tombola, and several sculptures by Tinguely and Ultvedt, including Tinguely's large grinder built on site. Music by Johann Sebastian Bach and radio broadcasts were played over the loudspeakers. At the apex of the round belly was a hole that visitors could stick their heads through to get a view of the exhibition hall. When the exhibition closed on 4 September, 1966, *She* was taken apart and the pieces were thrown away. It was important that nothing should remain, and in the catalogue it was established that "demolition was inscribed in her fate".[4]

The entire exhibition process was carefully documented. Photographers such as Hans Hammarskiöld and Lütfi Özkök were employed to photograph the work in progress. Their pictures were used in the catalogue and in the book *Hon – en historia* (She – A History) (1967), a publication that could be described as an archive exhibition in book form. Other photographs and reproductions were collected for *Hon – en historia*, including pictures of cathedrals and objects from art history, texts about Antoni Gaudí's and Facteur Cheval's remarkable buildings, excerpts from Sigmund Freud's *The Interpretation of Dreams* from 1899, in a text by Elias Cornell the cathedral is compared to a woman, and *La France Illustrée*. The book also includes a form of diary account of the exhibition's genesis, and a great many reviews from the Swedish and international press. Some texts occur in several translations, others only in the language in which they were originally published. Many of these articles are preserved in the substantial material relating to the production of *Hon – en historia* in the Moderna Museet archive.[5] In some cases, the photographs originally illustrating these reviews have been excluded in the book and replaced with other images. There are no comments on how the material in the book was selected, so it is up to the reader to determine the significance of the texts and pictures.

Esoteric currents

The title of the exhibition, *She – A Cathedral*, suggests links to the field of religion. Religion had a strong presence in the lives of Niki de Saint Phalle and Jean Tinguely. Niki de Saint Phalle attended a convent school. Her artistic practice is brimming with goddesses, cathedrals, dragons, angels and black madonnas, along with other symbols from religious and, more specifically, esoteric traditions. Her masterpiece, *Giardino dei Tarocchi* (1974–98), is a sculpture park based on the Tarot. The idea for the park came to her on a visit to Antoni Gaudí's *Park Güell* in Barcelona.[6] The numerous letters from Niki de Saint Phalle to Pontus Hultén preserved in the Moderna Museet archives, are full of words such as *magical*, *divine* and *energies*. In one of them, her spiritual convictions are particularly pronounced: "I hope you believe, like me, that life is not just an enormous accident. I hope you believe that there are mysterious

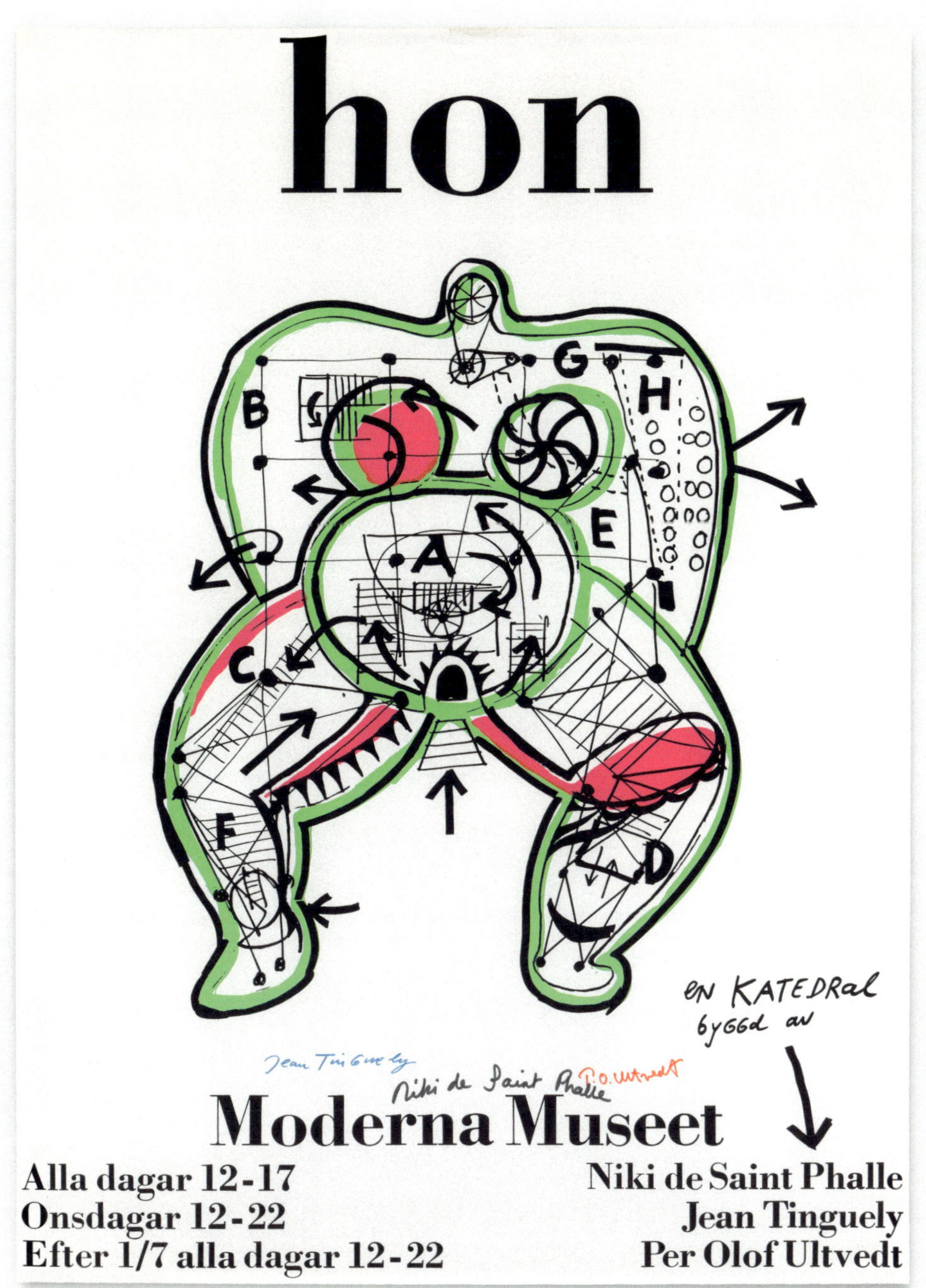

Poster for the exhibition *She – A Cathedral*, 1966, signed by the three artists Niki de Saint Phalle, Jean Tinguely and Per Olof Ultvedt

Per Olof Ultvedt during the construction
of *She – A Cathedral*, Moderna Museet, 1966

laws governing us, that we do not understand because we don't have access to them yet."[7]

Jean Tinguely, similarly, created artworks with religious or mythical connotations: labyrinths, cyclops and altar-like compositions. Some of the religious references stemmed from childhood memories: "Brought up a Catholic by nuns, he was under the thrall of the mystery and magic of the Mass."[8] In many of his works, he expressly refers to spiritually oriented artists such as Piet Mondrian and Kazimir Malevich. He was also close friends with Yves Klein, and an acquaintance of Jean Cocteau and Marcel Duchamp, all artists with profound knowledge in what has come to be known as Western esotericism.

The collective term *esotericism* includes Neo-Platonism, Hermeticism, astrology, magic, alchemy and the Kabbalah. All these different fields share a view of the world as enchanted. Esotericism can also be understood as that which constitutes the innermost core of every religion. The esoteric, inner side of religion is reserved for a spiritually enlightened minority, whereas the exoteric, outer side, is adapted to the level of consciousness of the general masses.[9] Mysticism and occultism strongly influenced many of the most famous modernist artists.[10] In the catalogue for the groundbreaking exhibition *The Spiritual in Art: Abstract Painting 1890–1985* (1986) it is emphasised that the development of abstract art was in fact inextricably linked to the spiritual ideas that flourished in Europe in the late-19th and early-20th centuries.[11] For example, the Bauhaus school, this flagship of modernism, was highly influenced by esoteric movements. Based on the concept of mediaeval guilds of builders and masons, its students were called apprentices. They were initiated into the secrets of crafts by masters, just like when the great cathedrals were built, or in the freemason lodges. Several of the artists who are now inscribed in the modernist canon, including Kazimir Malevich, Piet Mondrian, Paul Klee, Hilma af Klint, Wassily Kandinsky, Joseph Beuys and Yves Klein, belonged to esoteric circles such as the Rosicrucian Order, the Freemasons, the Theosophical Society and the Anthroposophical Society. The spiritual fountainheads of art and Western esotericism have long been relatively uncharted territory. One reason may be that the emerging fascism and Nazism of the 1930s and 1940s appropriated part of the esoteric ideas for their own purposes.[12] Over the past 25 years, however, there has been a resurgence of interest in research in this field.[13] There are also more exhibitions focusing on the spiritual in art.

Esoteric references in She – A Cathedral

When Niki de Saint Phalle and Jean Tinguely met in 1956, they introduced one another to esoterically influenced artistic practices:

> Ping pong. We were always playing – Ideas back and forth. When Jean and I started living together in 1960 he introduced me to Marcel Duchamp – Daniel Spoerri – Rauschenberg, Yves Klein and I introduced him to the world of the Facteur Cheval, Gaudi and the Watts Towers.[14]

She – A Cathedral includes several references to Marcel Duchamp. His works are teeming with symbols and words culled from the tradition of alchemy. Asked in an interview if his art should be regarded from an alchemical perspective, he replied:

> It is an Alchemical understanding. But don't stop there! [*Laughing.*] If we do, some will think I'm trying to turn lead into gold back in the kitchen. Alchemy is a kind of philosophy, a kind of thinking that leads to a way of understanding. We also may call this perspective "Tantric"(as Brâncuşi would say), or (as you like to say) "Perennial."[15]

As Duchamp's art became increasingly written about in the French press in the 1940s and early 1950s – and he himself made more frequent visits to his native France, granting more interviews and even creating exhibitions – he became an influential figure in Parisian intellectual circles.

The planned planetarium of ping-pong balls could be seen as a nod to the Milky Way (*la voie lactée*) in Marcel Duchamp's *The Bride Stripped Bare by Her Bachelors, Even* (1915–1923). Tinguely's vending machine is most certainly a Duchampian readymade, and the giant grinder that Tinguely created for the *She* interior can be interpreted as a reference to Duchamp's chocolate grinder. Not only does Duchamp's oeuvre contain countless esoteric references, but the links between Duchamp and *She – A Cathedral* can also be described as esoteric, in the sense of obscure or inaccessible to the general public. Without explicit explanations, this dimension of the exhibition was probably only perceived by a select circle of initiates. If contemporary critics are to be trusted, most people rather experienced *She – A Cathedral* like a visit to an amusement park.[16]

Above: The three artists in the exhibition *She – A Cathedral*, Moderna Museet, 1966. Below: Niki de Saint Phalle and Jean Tinguely during the installation of *She – A Cathedral*, 1966

More savvy visitors, however, could obtain guidance from Ulf Linde's review in *Dagens Nyheter*. It is reprinted in English, German and French at the beginning of the textual section of *Hon – en historia*, as if it were the official programme for the entire exhibition. Linde compares *She* with T. S. Eliot's *The Waste Land* (1922), a work that abounds in esoteric metaphors, and also highlights the significance of myths in the exhibition: "Yet this plastic richness never becomes an end in itself; everything is 'controlled' by the myth, by the original idea."[17]

She's roots in myth, religion and cult are revealed by many of the uncommented images and quotes reproduced in *Hon – en historia*, such as a photograph of Venus from Willendorf and a passage from a publication on the cathedral in Chartres. The Chartres text is about a sculpture of a mother goddess that was worshipped by the locals in Chartres and that was reportedly replaced with a Christian madonna.[18] Many critics mention the similarities between *She* and a goddess, including Ulf Linde, whose review in *Dagens Nyheter* refers to both Venus from Willendorf and "The Primordial Great Mother".[19]

Mother goddesses occur in myths all over the world. In all times, mankind has resorted to myths to see life in a wider context. The historian of religion Karen Armstrong writes that there are moments when we all, in one way or another, must embark on a voyage to a place we have never seen, to do something we have never done, and that myths can offer guidance in those moments.[20] Many myths follow a pattern – a hero or god must endure various ordeals and then returns to life with new-found wisdom.

The encounter with the mother goddess is usually described as the hero's last adventure and the highest form of enlightenment. In Syria, the mother goddess was shown as the consort of the supreme god El, or as Anat, El's daughter. She was called Inanna in Sumer in Mesopotamia, Isis in Egypt and became known in Greece as Hera, Demeter and Aphrodite. In Neolithic mythology, women were clearly seen as the stronger sex, in line with the feminist aspects of Niki de Saint Phalle's art. The Mesopotamian mother goddess Ereshkigal is queen over life and death and is often depicted in the act of giving birth. *She* was also in labour, with an incessant stream of visitors coming out of her vagina (and entering). The visitors of the exhibition participated in a form of drama and, like the mythical heroes, walked through the labyrinth and were born again. Another parallel is found in the Neolithic tunnels, which are believed to have been used ritually to evoke the feeling of entering the womb of Mother Earth and making a mystical passage back to the origins of life.[21] Niki de Saint Phalle claimed that visitors were not the same when they came out from *She* as when they entered.[22] In other words, she considered the visit to the exhibition to be a transformative experience, similar to other initiation rites. The transformation of visitors was also pointed out by a critic in the British leftist publication *The New Statesman* in 1966.[23]

Over the years, commentators have insisted that *She* should be interpreted as a sexually liberated woman or a prostitute.[24] A prostrate woman who allows countless visitors to penetrate her obviously invites that reading. Moreover, the motto *Honi soit qui mal y pense* (Shame on whoever thinks ill thereof) which was written on *She's* thigh is linked to prostitution.[25] Even if Niki de Saint Phalle herself admitted that *She* could be seen as a prostitute, she later commented that this had never been her intention:

> Wicked tongues said she was the biggest whore in the world [with] 100,000 visitors in three months. But for me she was never that. She was the incarnation of the ancient religion. Of the mother god[d]ess.[26]

It is also worth noting that *Honi soit qui mal y pense* is the motto of the Most Noble Order of the Garter. This is one of Britain's most prestigious orders, founded in 1348 by King Edward III. Its origins are debatable. One version claims that the Order of the Garter is linked to the legend of the Holy Grail, an exceedingly vital part of esoteric mysticism.[27]

The exhibition's most tangible religious reference is, of course, found in its title: *She – A Cathedral*.[28] According to the fabled alchemist Fulcanelli, Gothic cathedrals were built by mediaeval Freemasons to ensure that the Hermetic doctrines were passed on to a select group of initiates. The edifices were and are still today teeming with esoteric symbols and references, functioning as colossal books in stone. In *The Mysteries of the Cathedrals*, Fulcanelli writes:

> The cathedral is a work of *art goth* (Gothic art) or of *argot*, i.e. cant or slang. Moreover, dictionaries define argot as "a language peculiar to all individuals who wish to communicate their thoughts without being understood by outsiders."[29]

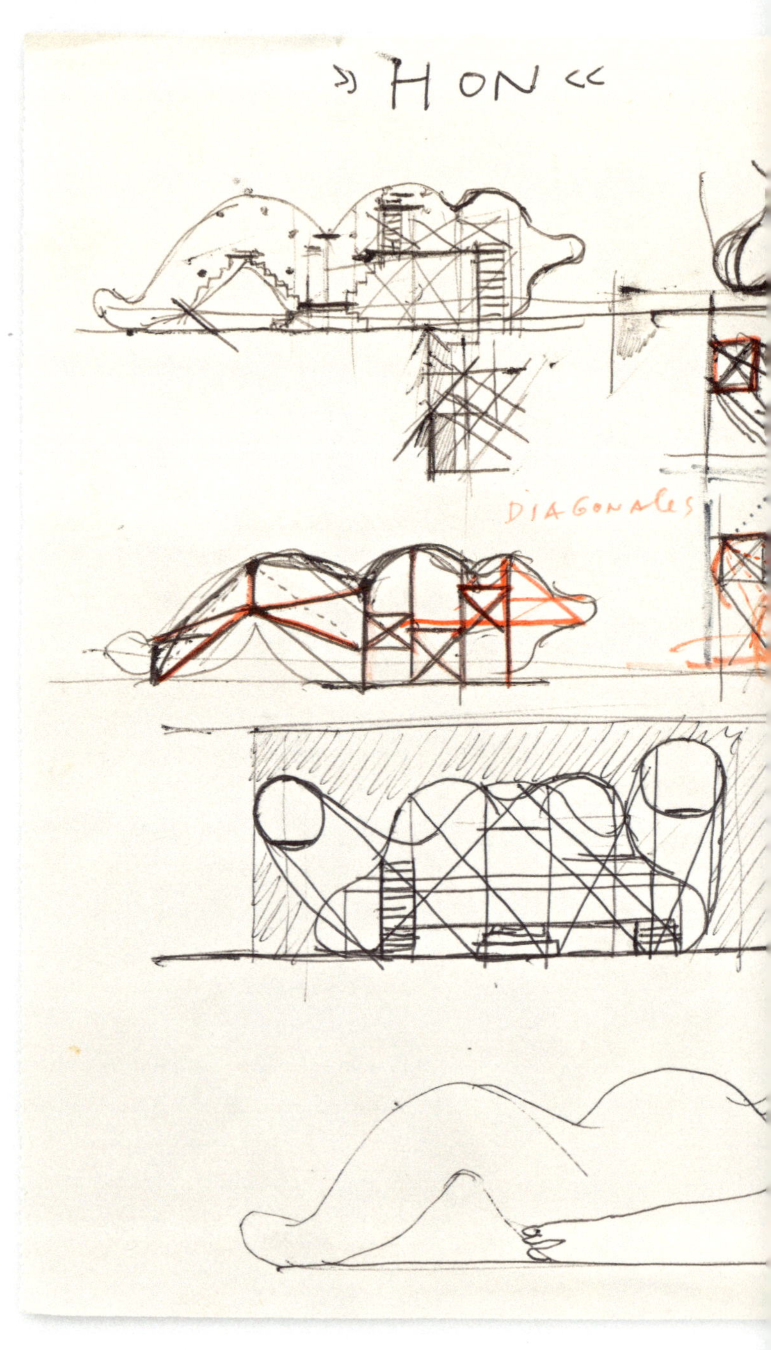

Jean Tinguely, *SHE* (1966),
sketch for the sculpture *She – A Cathedral*

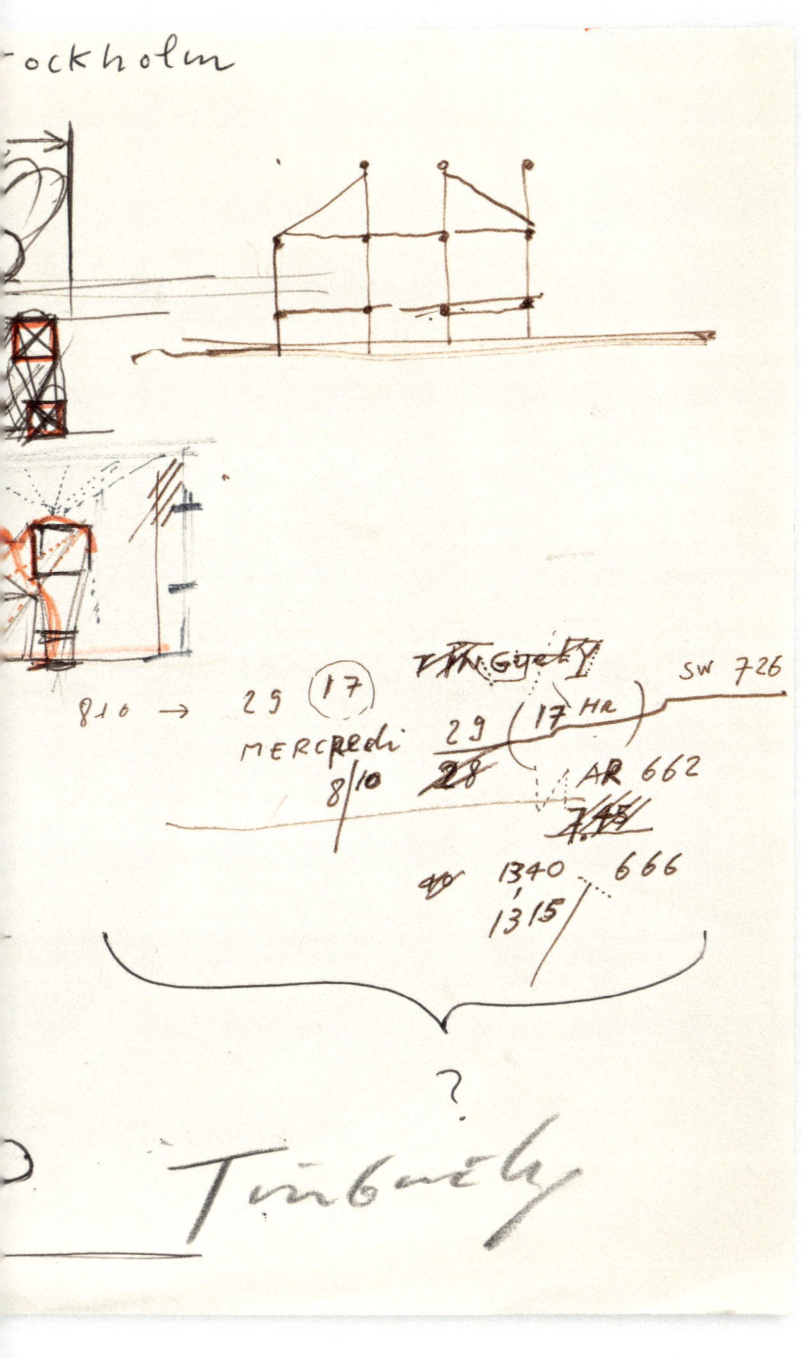
ockholm
Tinguely
SW 726
810 →
29 17
MERCREDI 29 17 HR
28
8/10
AR 662
666
1340
1315
?
Tinguely

Thus, the secrets are there for all to see in the cathedrals, but few can decode them.

Niki de Saint Phalle painted cathedrals early in her career. Although *Le Château du monstre et de la mariée* from around 1955 may depict a castle according to the title, the building strongly resembles a cathedral, with its rose window where a woman is giving birth. Thus, there were links between the cathedral and the woman giving birth early on in Niki de Saint Phalle's oeuvre. A later example is the plaster relief *La Cathédrale rouge* from 1962. Several texts and images in *Hon – en historia* refer to cathedrals, including Clas Brunius' exhibition review: "It certainly is a cathedral we enter. We sense the arched domes of the belly and breasts above us in the warm, dim light, like in a church from the time of the Crusades."[30] Adjoining the text is a picture of the crypt of the Crusader church in Acre, Israel. Another text that is quoted is *Det obeskrivliga huset* (The Indescribable House) by Elias Cornell, in which a cathedral is compared to a woman.[31]

Gothic cathedrals were often referred to as "palaces of the divine queen" or "our lady" (notre dame), since nearly all of them were dedicated to the Virgin Mary. Churches were frequently built on former sites for goddess worship. The Virgin Mary was also called *Ecclesia*, Church, alluding not only to the parish but to the church building itself. Even in ancient Egypt temples and their surrounding pillars were designated a female or male gender.[32]

The assumption that the creators of *She* were familiar with the fact that cathedrals are of the feminine gender is corroborated by Jean Tinguely's work *La Vittoria*, which was presented on 28 November, 1970. *La Vittoria* was a self-destructing 11-metre-tall machine in the form of a golden phallus with testicles bedecked with plastic fruits, which was inaugurated outside the cathedral in Milan. As it was unveiled, smoke and fireworks issued from the tip of the phallus, while loudspeakers blared out a drunken rendering of *O sole mio*. A more explicit enactment of the cathedral as a woman is hard to find. The planning of the work was partly secret, since Tinguely was reluctant to inform the authorities of the nature of his work. Before being unveiled, it was hidden behind great purple textiles adorned with the letters NR, as in Nouveau Réalisme. Pontus Hultén himself has mentioned the associations with the acronym INRI from the cross of Christ.[33]

The labyrinth as a structure and a symbol has a long history in religion, and the publication *Hon – en historia* includes several references to labyrinths. The working title of the exhibition was in fact "The Labyrinth" up to 1 April 1966. Earlier still, it had been called "The Emperor's New Clothing".[34] *She* was seen as a kind of sequel to the dynamic labyrinth *Dylaby* at the Stedelijk Museum in Amsterdam a few years previously.[35] Labyrinths have often been used to symbolise the spiritual voyage of heroes in myths. [36] An untranslated French essay from *The Situationist* that was reprinted in *Hon – en historia* relates how labyrinths have been found in the oldest Christian churches. They were appropriated as Christian symbols, while retaining their mystical quality as a model of the universe.[37] A text in Swedish printed alongside the French essay, gives a similar but not identical account:

> The road from a "dynamic labyrinth" to "She – A Cathedral" may seem long to a rational eye. In fact, it seems to follow a track that man has trod since time immemorial. The labyrinth is manifested in some form – danced, drawn, narrated or built – in all cultures, primitive or archaic, highly-evolved or modern. The labyrinth visualises notions of death and resurrection, of the transience and perpetual return of everything, of development and change. It is a model of the world and the human condition. There are labyrinths in the early Christian churches, but also in later cathedrals, including the cathedral in Chartres.[38]

As has now been shown, both the exhibition *She – A Cathedral* and the publication *Hon – en historia*, contain ample religious or spiritual references. The labyrinth, which can symbolise the meandering spiritual journey that each and everyone needs to embark upon in life, can be seen as an analogy to the exhibition itself. Only the visitor who was prepared to search for the hidden connections would reach the core of the exhibition and know its true meaning.

Success and well-kept secret

She – A Cathedral was seen by some 80,000 visitors in the three months the exhibition was open.[39] The Swedish and international press covered the event profusely. Even 55 years after it was shown, it is the subject of analysis and discussion. The exhibition that preceded *She* at Moderna Museet was *Inner and Outer Space*, a comprehensive presentation of Kazimir Malevich, Naum Gabo and Yves Klein, together with 35 works by 35 other artists. According to

Pontus Hultén, *Inner and Outer Space* "inclined strongly towards mysticism of the transcendental kind."[40] *She*, at first glance, was the polar opposite of Yves Klein's spiritual exploration of colour and Malevich's terse suprematism; *She* was immediate and inviting, playful and engaging. But, as Patrik Andersson has demonstrated, the more inaccessible *Inner and Outer Space* prepared the ground for *She – A Cathedral*.[41] The latter consolidated the outer with the inner, the popular with the esoteric, in an unprecedented way.[42] For Pontus Hultén, irrational and rational were not mutually exclusive concepts:

> Why has Niki de Saint Phalle's work been considered marginal by some? For several reasons, most of them without interest: anti-feminism, indifference, prejudice, lack of curiosity. There are, nevertheless, more profound reasons: science and rationalism have dominated our century. In spite of the marvelous clairvoyance of Dada; in spite of the inroads of the Surrealists in areas usually inaccessible to the conscious mind; in spite of Cubism and in spite of our fundamental individualism, the exaltation of the joy of life of which Matisse was the master is no longer fashionable.[43]

A cornerstone of social democratic cultural policy in the 1960s was that art should be accessible to the broader public and contribute to eradicating class divides.[44] In 1966, the same year as the exhibition at Moderna Museet, Pierre Bourdieu and Alain Darbel published *The Love of Art. European Art Museums and Their Public*, a sociological study of museum audiences. It included suggestions for making museums more appealing to the lower and middle classes. Several of the ideas expressed in *The Love of Art* were realised in *She – A Cathedral*.[45] Striving for a new and broader audience from different social strata was a current tendency in the mid-1960s, and this resonated with Pontus Hultén. Johan Huizinga's oft-quoted book *Homo Ludens* (1938) focused on play as the principle that underpins creativity. Play and the visitors' participation were central to several of the projects that the artists behind *She* were involved with in the 1950s and 1960s.[46] In the process of creating *She*, the curators and artists envisioned "a form of theatre, where the audience would be provoked into participating in the performance".[47] *She* could be described as a drama without a stage, where visitors took the place of actors. This is clear, not least, if we consider that conversations between people in the lovers' seat were recorded with hidden

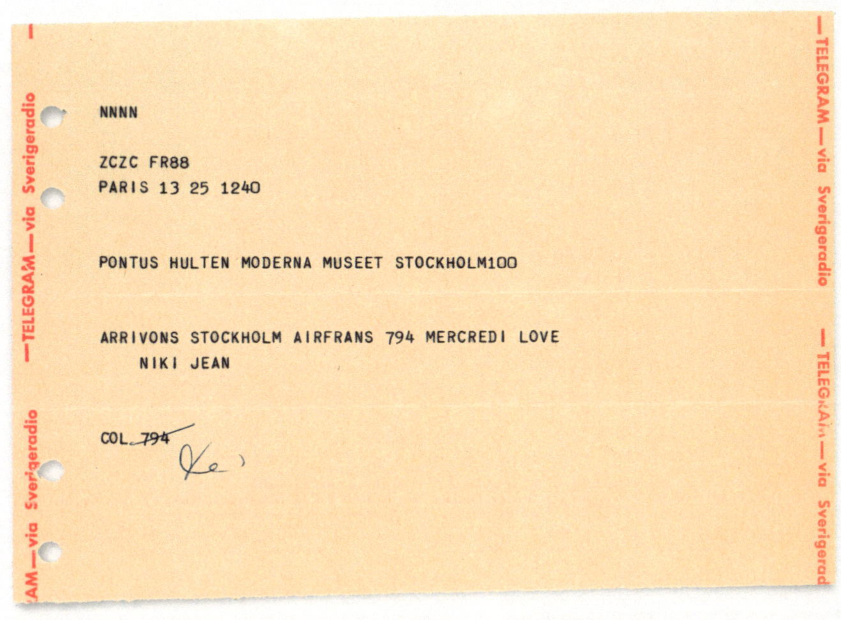
NNNN

ZCZC FR88
PARIS 13 25 1240

PONTUS HULTEN MODERNA MUSEET STOCKHOLM100

ARRIVONS STOCKHOLM AIRFRANS 794 MERCREDI LOVE
NIKI JEAN

COL 794

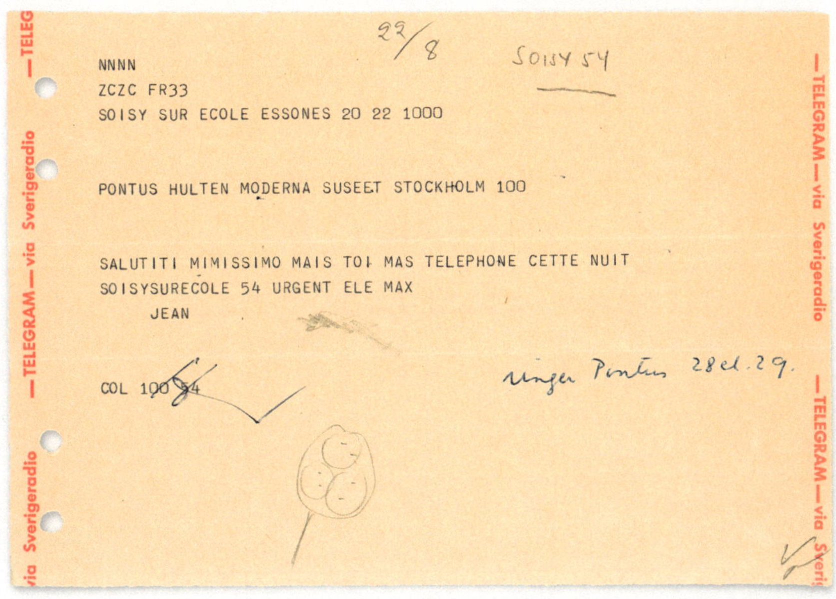
NNNN
ZCZC FR33
SOISY SUR ECOLE ESSONES 20 22 1000

PONTUS HULTEN MODERNA SUSEET STOCKHOLM 100

SALUTITI MIMISSIMO MAIS TOI MAS TELEPHONE CETTE NUIT
SOISYSURECOLE 54 URGENT ELE MAX
JEAN

COL 100 54

Above: Telegram from Niki de Saint Phalle and Jean Tinguely to Pontus Hultén, 1966. Below: Telegram from Jean Tinguely to Pontus Hultén, 1966

Visitors at the exhibition *She – A Cathedral*,
Moderna Museet, 1966

microphones and broadcast through loudspeakers in the bar.[48] It is not clear whether anyone ever mentioned that this arrangement could be problematic in the sense that it invaded the visitors' personal integrity. Whatever the case, it is hard to banish the feeling that visitors to the exhibition were used as pawns in a game, involuntary walk-ons in a drama directed by the curator and artists.

Pontus Hultén was well-aware of the importance of offering visitors some type of educational activity. In 1956, two years before Moderna Museet opened, he stated:

> … a work of art is not an isolated object, but has numerous connections: in film, in literature, yes, even in politics or purely socially. Gone are the days when a museum could hang paintings on its walls and expect people to immediately show an interest. People want to know more in order to understand better and get more out of their art experience: that is the line we must pursue at a modern museum.[49]

Under Hultén, Moderna Museet earned a reputation for being both open and accessible. Visitors were offered art exhibitions, readings, guided tours, film screenings, lectures and discussions, along with events especially for kids and youngsters.[50]

In *She*, as in *Dylaby* at the Stedelijk Museum a few years earlier, visitors could move around inside the art and interact with it by, for instance, getting something in the bar, poking their heads out through the navel of *She*, or smashing bottles in Tinguely's sculpture. Hostesses were recruited to make visitors feel comfortable and ensure that the place did not get too crowded:

> It is decided that the relationships between "She" and the public, whose character one dares not predict, shall be in the hands of special "She" hostesses. Hostess uniforms will be purchased, and also traffic lights regulating the potential crowds.[51]

In a text that appears to be a transcribed conversation or recording in which Pontus Hultén tries to establish a timeline for the *She* process based on photographs, he talks about the *She* hostesses:

> … and then we got these hostess uniforms, nobody knew how things would develop, how people would react, we were concerned that there might be crowding, and that the hostesses would have to ensure that there weren't

> too many people in there, and that was when the green and red lights were added, there were a lot of fears that there would be so many people in there that it would be hazardous, the whole system with loudspeakers, [illegible, probably for example] The She hostesses were devised through speculation, mainly mine perhaps, about what could happen.[52]

Thus, the hostesses were there primarily to maintain order, not to inform, at least not according to this statement.

She invited concrete interaction between art and visitors, regardless of their particular background. But physical access says nothing about how accessible the ideas underlying the exhibition were to visitors. The catalogue provided opportunities for them to acquaint themselves with the actual production of the exhibition and biographical data about the artists. There were also information sheets where they could read the following:

> SHE – a cathedral is also something much more important than a big woman figure. SHE functions as a very irrational summing-up, a conclusion, a labyrinth of many sentiments and milieus. SHE could be seen as a representation of our life, in anthropomorphic form. A synthesis of facts, dreams, actions. Many visitors experience SHE very directly, in a [sic!] unsophisticated way, as an enormous happening, engaging and amusing.[53]

The Museum was obviously adamant to point out that there was a deeper meaning to the exhibition but did not state what it was. At least not in this information sheet. A journalist reporting on the exhibition for the men's magazine *Mayfair* in December 1966 seems to have belonged to the above-mentioned unsophisticated group, as he notes: "The symbolism of 'She' was hidden. So expertly that I must confess I never found it."[54]

Those who were interested in the symbolism but lacked the prior knowledge required to decode it could find possible interpretations in press reviews of the exhibition, which, as we have seen, offered associations to both fertility goddesses, mediaeval cathedrals and a critique of consumerism.[55] Interestingly, all of the reviews, images and essays reproduced in the book *Hon – en historia* are uncommented by the editors. Readers are left to decide for themselves how relevant they were, an approach which can appear either generous or arrogant. The disparity between the critics' interpretations and

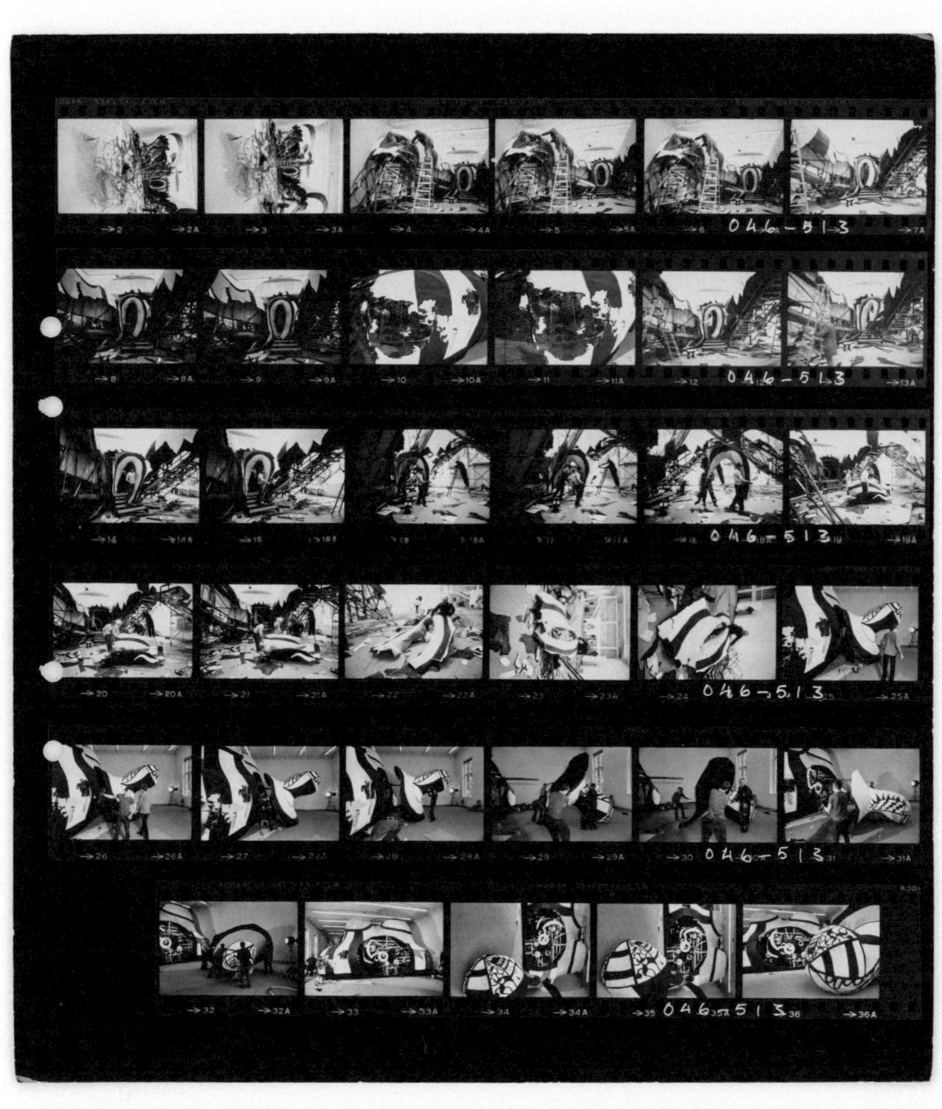

Contact sheet from the demolition of
She – A Cathedral at Moderna Museet, 1966

how visitors experienced the exhibition, between the initiated and the uninformed, is highlighted in a feature in *Expressen:*

> – But this is not art, although it is fun and very entertaining. And it's great that this is offered by museums, which are usually so boring.
>
> …
>
> Expressen said:
>
> – Nevertheless, "SHE" is "an intriguing and profoundly poetic work" (DN). If you look carefully in there, you will find "the gesture of procreation", not to mention "pre-Christian fertility cult". There is also a "room for the desire of the lonely to be desired" (all from DN).
>
> – Really, said Young Sweden, Is it really that boring?
>
> – Wasn't it supposed to be fun?
>
> – Yes, said Expressen, who knows the vibrant director of Moderna Museet, Yes, that was probably also the idea.[56]

While *Expressen* poked fun at *Dagens Nyheter*'s (*DN*) pretentious reading of the exhibition, the ignorance of the general public seems to have been subject to some laughs at the museum. Archive material relating to the production of *Hon – en historia* includes a transcribed conversation between a cab driver and a museum staff member (possibly Hultén himself). The driver complains about not being able to understand modern art, which doesn't resemble anything in real life. He is represented as being unsophisticated:

> M [Me]: What is art?
>
> C [Cab driver]: Well, Picasso, that's not art either, an eye here, a nose there, and an ear somewhere, I could paint that.
>
> M: Have you tried? So, what is art?
>
> C: Well, that Van Gogh, and whatever their names are, all those old, real artists, that's art, when they made people the way they look, and trees and landscapes the way they look …[57]

This passage was not included in the final publication, but the fact that it was even considered reveals an attitude that does not sit particularly well with Hultén's ambition that Moderna Museet should be a museum for everyone.

The very definition of esotericism – that all religions have an official side and a hidden side that is reserved for a select few – could also be applied to *She – A Cathedral*. The exhibitors managed the feat of appealing to both the broader public and a small circle of initiates. By publishing the learned analyses in *Hon – en historia* together with pictures of visitors blissfully enjoying the spectacle, and without further comment on the disparate approaches, they succeeded in maintaining the integrity of the exhibition even to posterity. The references to esoteric tradition, to myth and religion, are hidden in plain sight, in both the exhibition and the subsequent publication.

1. For feminist readings, see, for instance: Gudrun Ekeflo, "Varför är HON en katedral", *Hon – en historia*, eds. Barbro Sylwan, K. G. Hultén, John Melin and Anders Österlin, Stockholm: Moderna Museet, 1967, p. 155; Naja Rasmussen, "Niki de Saint Phalle – Feminist and Femme Fatale", and Camilla Jalving, "The Giant Woman in Stockholm", *Niki de Saint Phalle* (exh. cat.), Ishøj: Arken Museum of Modern Art, 2015, pp. 51–84; Susan Jenkins, "Niki de Saint Phalle", *Wack! Art and the Feminist Revolution* (exh. cat.), ed. Lisa Gabrielle Mark, Los Angeles: The Museum of Contemporary Art, 2007, and Annika Öhrner, "Niki de Saint Phalle Playing with the Feminine in the Male Factory: Hon – en katedral", *Stedelijk Studies*, issue no. 7, 2018, https://stedelijkstudies.com/journal/niki-de-saint-phalle-playing-with-the-feminine-in-the-male-factory-hon-en-katedral/ (23 August, 2022). Andreas Gedin highlights the mediaeval carnival tradition in relation to *SHE*, in Andreas Gedin, *Pontus Hultén, Hon & Moderna,* Stockholm: Bokförlaget Langenskiöld, 2016, pp. 215–217. Benoît Antille discusses the exhibition in light of cultural policy at the time, in Benoît Antille, "'HON – en katedral'. Behind Pontus Hultén's Theatre of Inclusiveness", *Afterall*, no. 32, spring 2013, pp. 72–81. For a broader discussion on the performative aspects of *She – A Cathedral*, see, for instance Patrik Andersson, *Euro-Pop. The Mechanical Bride Stripped Bare in Stockholm, Even* (diss.), Vancouver: University of British Columbia, 2001, pp. 175–197.

2. Annika Öhrner, *Stedelijk Studies*, issue no. 7, 2018. However, both Ulf Linde's and Richard Boston's reviews of the exhibition refer to the planetarium in one of the breasts of the sculpture. Ulf Linde, "En väldig skapelse", *Dagens Nyheter*, 4 June, 1966, reprinted in *Hon – en historia*, 1967, p. 138. Richard Boston, "Hon", *The New Statesman*, 22 July, 1966. MMA MA F1a:32.

3. Each "forgery" bore the word "fake", and all the signatures were misspelled, see *Hon – en historia*, 1967, p. 103. Two of these works are now in the Moderna Museet collection: a "fake" Paul Klee (MOM/2005/465) and a "fake" Jean Fautrier (MOM/2015/102).

4. *Hon – en historia*, 1967, p. 2. It should be added that not all parts of *Hon* were, in fact, destroyed. The head was preserved and presented in numerous exhibitions, including the recent *Remembering She – A Cathedral* in the Pontus Hultén Study Gallery at Moderna Museet on 3 June, 2018 – 10 March, 2019. Furthermore, some colourful pieces from the exterior of the sculpture were sold together with the exhibition catalogue in the museum bookshop, in a limited edition of 150 copies. This was confirmed in conversation with Susanna Rydén Danckwardt, a long-term employee at the museum, 13 January, 2022.

5. See Press clippings. MMA MA F1a:32.

6. Naja Rasmussen, *Niki de Saint Phalle*, 2015, pp. 24–25.

7. Letter of condolence from Niki de Saint Phalle to Pontus Hultén and Anna-Lena Wibom, 2 October, 1998. MMA PHA 5.1.36.

8. Niki de Saint Phalle, manuscript "JEAN", p. 4. MMA PHA 5.1.41.

9. For further studies of the history of Western esotericism, see, for instance, Wouter J. Hanegraaff, *Esotericism and the Academy. Rejected*

Knowledge in Western Culture, Cambridge: Cambridge University Press, 2012; Wouter J. Hanegraaff, *Western Esotericism: A Guide for the Perplexed*, London and New York: Bloomsbury Academic, 2013; Nicholas Goodrick-Clarke, *The Western Esoteric Traditions: A Historical Introduction*, Oxford: Oxford University Press, 2008.

10. See, for instance, Maurice Tuchman, "Hidden meanings in abstract art", ed. Maurice Tuchman, *The Spiritual in Art: Abstract Painting 1890–1985*, New York: Abbeville Press, pp. 17–62; Roger Lipsey, *The Spiritual in Twentieth-Century Art*, Mineola, New York: Dover Publications, inc., 2011; Peter Cornell, *Den hemliga källan. Om initiationsmönster i konst, litteratur och politik*, Hedemora: Gidlunds bokförlag, 1988. The historian of ideas Kjell Lekeby highlights the alchemist Fulcanelli's alleged apprentice Eugène Canseliet as essential to the interest in alchemy that blossomed in the 1960s and 1970s, especially in France. Canseliet was also an acquaintance of André Breton. See Kjell Lekeby, "Fulcanelli i Sverige" in Fulcanelli, *Katedralernas mysterium* (1929), Malmö: Vertigo förlag, 2013, p. 12.

11. Maurice Tuchman, *The Spiritual in Art,* 1986, p. 17.

12. Ibid., p. 18.

13. See, for instance, Mark Sedgewick, *Against the Modern World: Traditionalism and the Secret Intellectual History of the Twentieth Century*, Oxford: Oxford University Press, 2004, p. 13. The legacy of Édouard Schuré (1841–1929), French writer and esoteric, Mircea Eliade (1907–1986), Romanian religious historian at the Sorbonne after the Second World War, and in Chicago from 1956, and the French historian of religion Antoine Faivre (1934–2021) is maintained by many scholars today, including Wouter J. Hanegraaff, professor of the History of Hermetic Philosophy and Related Currents at Amsterdam University. Courses in the history of Western esotericism are offered all over Europe, including at the Universities of Uppsala, Gothenburg and Stockholm.

14. Niki de Saint Phalle, manuscript "Collaboration", p. 4. MMA PHA 5.1.41.

15. John F. Moffitt, *Alchemist of the Avant-Garde: The Case of Marcel Duchamp*, Albany: State University of New York Press, 2003, p. 9.

16. See, for instance, "The Ultimate She", *Time*, 17 June, 1966 (writer unknown, reprinted in *Hon – en historia*, 1967, p. 154), and Folke Edwards, "Lustiga huset", *Sydsvenska Dagbladet*, 15 June, 1966.

17. Ulf Linde, "A Giant Among Women", *Dagens Nyheter*, 4 June, 1966, reprinted in *Hon – en historia*, 1967, p. 140.

18. *Hon – en historia*, 1967, p. 142. The Madonna sculpture referred to in the essay could be the famous Black Madonna in Chartres. The nascence of black madonnas is debated, but one theory claims that a group of black madonnas were, in fact, originally pre-Christian goddesses, such as Isis. To appease the masses when the new religion was introduced, these goddesses were remodelled into madonnas that were acceptable to both heathens and Christians. It is worth noting that black madonnas and references to black madonnas are also found in several other works by Niki de Saint Phalle.

19. Ulf Linde, *Dagens Nyheter*, 4 June, 1966.

20. Karen Armstrong, *A Short History of Myth*, Edinburgh: Canongate, 2005, p. 37.

21. Armstrong refers to a note in Mircea Eliade's book *Myths, Dreams and Mysteries*, published in French in 1957. It is worth noting that Pontus Hultén's library includes another title by Eliade, namely *Méphistophélès et l'androgyne*, Paris: Éditions Gallimard, 1962.

22. *Niki de Saint Phalle et le projet Hon*, an archival short film with an interview: https://www.youtube.com/watch?v=jNfQt2FsUD4 (23 August, 2022).

23. "No one who has entered her will ever be quite the same again." Richard Boston, "Hon", *The New Statesman*, 22 July, 1966. This sentence is reprinted in bold type in *Hon – en historia*, p. 169, with no explanation as to why.

24. For examples, see Staffan Roos, "Hon – ett ätbart fnask", *Helsingborgs Dagblad*, 17 July, 1966; Arthur Secunda and Jan Thunholm, "Everyman's Girl", reprinted in *Hon – en historia*, 1967, pp. 150–151; Andreas Gedin, *Pontus Hultén, Hon & Moderna*, 2016, pp. 196–197, and Benoît Antille, "'HON – en katedral'. Behind Pontus Hultén's Theatre of Inclusiveness", *Afterall*, no. 32, spring 2013, pp. 72–81.

25. Andreas Gedin, *Pontus Hultén, Hon & Moderna*, 2016, p. 197.

26. The quote is from Niki de Saint Phalle, manuscript "The HON", p. 13. MMA PHA 5.1.41. See also the documentary film *Niki de Saint Phalle & Jean Tinguely – Les Bonnie & Clyde de l'Art* by Louise Faure and Anne Julien, 2009, https://www.youtube.com/watch?v=3y-I-KpxiG8 (23 August, 2022).

27. Albert B. Friedman and Richard H. Osberg, *The Journal of American Folklore*, vol. 90, no. 357, 1977, p. 314 (pp. 301–315). Incidentally, Niki de Saint Phalle was asked in the 1950s if she could play Guinevere in Robert Bresson's film *Lancelot du Lac* (a drama about the legend of the Holy Grail and the Knights of the Round Table), but the part went to Niki's daughter more than 20 years later. See Tony Pipolo, *Robert Bresson. A Passion for Film*, Oxford: Oxford University Press, 2010, note 2, p. 391.

28. Replacing the word "cathedral" with "history" in the title of the publication documenting the exhibition seems only fitting in this perspective. In a letter to Barbro Sylwan, Hultén writes: "That thing about She – A Cathedral A History [arrow pointing at 'Cathedral', and the word 'crossed out'] seems to have got lost. Was it dropped? How about having it on the spine of the book ???? It should be crossed out in red. red. in that case with 'a history' also in red." Letter from Pontus Hultén to Barbro Sylwan, Amsterdam, 5 May, 1967. MMA MA F1a:32.

29. Fulcanelli, *Katerdralernas mysterium*, 1929/2013, p. 44. In argot, words are used that sound the same but shift the meaning, for instance *art scénique* (stage art) and *arsenic*, or *même* (even) and *m'aime* (loves me), a device Marcel Duchamp used profusely in his work titles. The Moderna Museet collection includes an undated drawing (MOM/2005/271) with the words "Tu est moi" by Niki de Saint Phalle. *Tu est moi* is an ungrammatical phrase in French that means "you is me" but is pronounced the same as

tu et moi (you and me) and *tuez moi* (kill me). A collage by Niki de Saint Phalle in the collection of Princeton University Art Museum has the same title. The phrase "You are Me" recurs in various varieties in esoteric contexts to establish that we are all one and the same, parts of a oneness.

30. Clas Brunius, "Moderna museets senaste: Jättekvinna på rygg", *Expressen*, 3 June, 1966, reprinted in *Hon – en historia*, 1967, p. 144.

31. Elias Cornell, "Det obeskrivliga huset", *Studiekamraten*, no. 4, 1966, reprinted in *Hon – en historia*, 1967, p. 142.

32. Barbara G. Walker, *The Woman's Dictionary of Symbols and Sacred Objects*, New York: Harper Collins, 1988, pp. 87–88. Andreas Gedin, on the other hand, claims that the cathedral is a patriarchal structure, and that *She* is a parody of that masculine building. He writes: "The patriarchal, religious architectural monument is replaced by a reclining, spreadeagled giant woman. The cathedral towers, which rise to the heavens above the city's rooftops and form its unique skyline are represented in this supine cathedral by an open vagina, the exalted is the base." Andreas Gedin, *Pontus Hultén, Hon & Moderna*, 2016, p. 279.

33. Pontus Hultén, *Tinguely* (exh. cat.), Paris: Éditions du Centre Georges Pompidou, 1988, p. 196.

34. Letter from K. G. Hultén to the engineer Harry Mattsson, 1 April, 1966, and letter from Pontus Hultén to the director Yngve Smedberg, Strand Hotell, Stockholm, 15 March, 1966. MMA MA F1a:32,

35. *Dylaby* was shown at the Stedelijk Museum in Amsterdam from 30 August to 30 September, 1962.

36. *Book of Symbols: Reflections on Archetypal Images*, eds. Ami Ronnberg and Kathleen Martin, Cologne: Taschen, 2010, p. 714.

37. "Le labyrinthe dont on trouve le dessin dans les mosaïques des pavés des églises chrétiennes les plus anciennes, devient symbole chrétien, paradigme religieux, tout en conservant son caractère mythique, c'est-à-dire son sens de 'modèle' du monde." From "Le labyrinthe de la Cathédrale de Chartres", *The Situationist*, no. 4, 1963, reprinted in *Hon – en historia*, 1967, p. 156.

38. *Hon – en historia*, 1967, p. 156.

39. *Statens konstsamlingars tillväxt och förvaltning 1966*, Meddelanden från Nationalmuseum, no. 91, 1967, p. 25.

40. Pontus Hultén, "Avslutande inledning", *Den inre och den yttre rymden. En utställning rörande en universell konst*, eds. Karin Bergqvist Lindegren and Pontus Hultén, Moderna Museet exhibition catalogue no. 51, Stockholm: Moderna Museet, 1965, unpaginated.

41. Patrik Andersson writes: "Considering the mythical, even spiritual, side of this move toward an unknown fourth dimension, we can say that Moderna Museet found itself born again. It was now ready to reconcile inner individual spaces with outer social space by constructing the spectacular *Hon – en katedral*, a cathedral built with Duchampian irony and wit." Patrik Andersson, "The Inner and the Outer Space. Rethinking movement in art", *Pontus Hultén and Moderna Museet. The Formative Years*, eds.

Anna Tellgren and Anna Lundström, Stockholm: Moderna Museet and London: Koenig Books, 2017, p. 58.

42. Andreas Gedin writes: "*She – A Cathedral* successfully summed up Hultén's approach to art, cultural policy and democracy. It included the amalgamation of avant-garde and transparency that Hultén felt was crucial. Not only was *She* a meta-museum, but also a utopian ideal museum: the project was advanced to the initiated, it challenged conventions but was still interactive and easy to grasp for the interested without too much prior knowledge, including kids." Andreas Gedin, *Pontus Hultén, Hon & Moderna*, 2016, p. 140.

43. Pontus Hultén, "Working with Fury and with Pleasure", *Niki de Saint Phalle*, Stuttgart: Hatje, 1992, p. 17.

44. See, for instance, David Rynell Åhlén, *Samtida konst på bästa sändningstid* (diss.), Mediehistoriskt arkiv no. 31, Lund: Lund University, 2016, and Benoît Antille, *Afterall*, 2013. Antille writes that one of the Museum's ambitions with the exhibition was to attract the working class, which only constituted three per cent of visitors in 1966.

45. One proposal was that the art presented in the exhibitions should relate to everyday life, that music should be played in the museum halls, and that hosts should be available to help visitors feel comfortable in the museum. See Pierre Bourdieu and Alain Darbel with Dominique Schnapper, *The Love of Art. European Art Museums and Their Public,* transl. by Caroline Beatty and Nick Merriman, Cambridge: Polity Press, 1991. Also Benoît Antille, *Afterall*, 2013, p. 75.

46. In the catalogue for the Tinguely exhibition at the Stedelijk Museum in 2017, the practice of Tinguely is described: "And what about his groundbreaking exhibition practices, with which he transformed the 'elitist' museum into an interactive, public-friendly space, lending new dimensions to our conception of what art is, both aesthetically and socially?" It is reasonable to assume that neither Hultén nor Tinguely could claim sole responsibility for this transformation, but that they each contributed to the new approach to museums. See Margriet Schavemaker, Barbara Til, Beat Wismer, "Jean Tinguely: An Introduction", *Jean Tinguely* (exh. cat.), eds. Margriet Schavemaker, Barbara Til and Beat Wismer, Cologne: Verlag der Buchhandlung Walther König, 2016, p. 9.

47. *Hon – en katedral*, 1967, p. 4.

48. Recording the voices of visitors with microphones and broadcasting them elsewhere in the exhibition had already been done at the exhibition *This Is Tomorrow* at Whitechapel Gallery in London in 1956. See Mark Wigley, "'The Museum Is the Massage'. Between the Discursive and the Immersive", *Stedelijk Studies,* issue no. 4, 2016, http://www.stedelijkstudies.com/journal/discursive-versus-immersive-museum-massage/ (23 August, 2022).

49. Pontus Hultén in "Liten intervju", *Dagens Nyheter*, 1956, quoted in Andreas Gedin, *Pontus Hultén, Hon & Moderna*, 2016, p. 125.

50. For further discussion on this, see Ylva Hillström, "Parallel Stories. Educational activities in Moderna Museet's early years", *Pontus Hultén and Moderna Museet. The Formative Years*, Stockholm, 2017, pp. 149–172.

51. *Hon – en historia*, p. 104 and confirmed in conversation with Mette Prawitz, who was employed by the museum at the time, 13 January, 2022.

52. Pontus Hultén, ”Pontus om Hon”. MMA MA F1a:3.

53. Exhibition text dated August 1966. MMA MA F1a:32. There would also have been texts in Swedish in the exhibition, but no copy of these is preserved in the archive. “Texts to guide visitors inside ‘She’ are stencilled.” Note in *Hon – en historia*, 1967, p. 98.

54. Sam Heppner, “Sweden – Land of a Million Girls”, *Mayfair*, December, 1966, p. 42.

55. Selected reviews are reprinted in *Hon – en historia*, 1967.

56. Lars Widding, “HON – ‘sköte-synd’ på Moderna?”, *Expressen*, 8 June, 1966.

57. Unsigned text dated 30 March, 1967. MMA MA F1a:32.

TRYING TO FACE THE STORM AGAIN

Pontus Hultén during the installation of the work *Fakir in ¾ Time* (1968) by Lucy Jackson Young (artist) and Niels O. Young (engineer) in the exhibition *The Machine*, The Museum of Modern Art, New York, 1968

Trying to Face the Storm Again.
Pontus Hultén's The Machine as Seen at the End of the Mechanical Age

Lars Bang Larsen

With more than "200 works of art and related objects" *The Machine* opened on 27 November, 1968, at New York's Museum of Modern Art (MoMA), where Pontus Hultén had realised it with the assistance of curator Jennifer Licht and her assistant Jean-Edith Weiffenbach.[1] During 1969, Hultén's New York guest appearance was followed by *The Machine*'s tour to the University of St. Thomas, in Houston, and the San Francisco Museum of Modern Art in what was as a major overseas manifestation of art histories and curatorial strategies that had been developed at Stockholm's Moderna Museet during his directorship.

MoMA director René d'Harnoncourt had initiated talks with Hultén in 1965 with an American version of *Movement in Art*, the seminal group show that Hultén co-curated with Jean Tinguely and Daniel Spoerri at Moderna Museet in 1961, in mind.[2] Even though Tinguely and other proponents of kinetic art also figured prominently in *The Machine*, MoMA ended up getting an entirely different package – namely, an early curatorial engagement with the relation between art and technology in the context of Western modernity, a history onto which *The Machine* took a long view *as seen at the end of the mechanical age*, the exhibition's subtitle announced.

Although one in this might pick up an echo of Walter Benjamin's famous essay "The Work of Art in the Age of Mechanical Reproduction" (1935), Hultén doesn't reference Benjamin (even if themes of speed and reproducibility are central to *The Machine* too); perhaps because he was concerned with "comments on technology by artists of the Western world" rather than with the effects of industrialism's image technologies on the work of art.[3] Hultén's exhibition can perhaps be compared with Benjamin's angel of history, from his equally famous essay "Theses on the Philosophy of History" (1940), with its face that was "turned towards the past": this because *The Machine*, by pointing to a historical rupture in which the industrial machine is no longer a given, while at the same time placing its emphasis on machine technology rather than on what comes after, "fixedly contemplat[es]" the past it is moving away from, its back turned to the future that "the storm of progress" is propelling it into.[4] Thus the exhibition proclaimed the new but mainly offered the old, and its attachment to a mechanical paradigm seems to have refused it access to discourse formations in its own era. Also other exhibitions at the time, such as Harald Szeemann's *Junggesellenmaschinen/Les machines célibataires* (1975), searched for a breakthrough to postmodernism through machinic imaginaries.

This essay is based on consultations with the Pontus Hultén archive at Moderna Museet that contains materials related to the making of the show at MoMA, the exhibition catalogue, and its tour.[5] The many ambitious loans of artworks and artefacts that *The Machine* required, and Hultén's long distance work from Stockholm during the preparation of the show, generated much correspondence, large portions of which is also available alongside the theoretical and art historical literature that Hultén consulted. In terms of both visual documentation and critical reception, it is the New York version of the show that is most comprehensively represented in Hultén's archive at Moderna Museet, and that has informed the following discussion of *The Machine* through aspects of its exhibition history.

"This show is doomed!" – The making of The Machine

> [T]echnology today is undergoing a critical transition. We are surrounded by the outward manifestations of the culmination of the mechanical age. Yet, at the same time, the mechanical machine – which can most easily be defined as an imitation of our muscles – is losing its dominating position among the tools of mankind; while electronic and chemical devices – which imitate the processes of the brain and the nervous system – are becoming increasingly important.[6]

Calling up a vast thematic domain, *The Machine* eschewed a formalist art history for a focus on mechanical mobility and image making that included feats of engineering alongside artworks. In the exhibition catalogue, a semiotic system reflected this interdisciplinarity: a spiralling arrow for "art", a light bulb for "invention", a small oldfashioned camera for "camera", a small vehicle for "car", thus distinguishing between artefacts while underscoring the juxtaposition – or near-levelling? – of artworks and machines. Specifically, the technical organisation of human movement and gaze was represented by an array of vehicles and various photographic

Exhibition catalogue for *The Machine as Seen at the End of the Mechanical Age*, 1968

apparatuses, including outlandish 19th-century patents such as Étienne-Jules Marey's "camera gun".

Correspondence between Stockholm and New York speaks of the exhibition's troubled genesis. Often provisional replies to loan requests that Jennifer Licht forwarded to Hultén are annotated with her comments, "Doesn't look good", "Reluctance to lend", or even, "This show is doomed!"[7] In spite of adversity, *The Machine* ended up spanning half a millennium's worth of cultural production with spectacular loans. On the side of art history, the show's avant-garde spine included works by artists such as El Lissitzky, Hannah Höch, Umberto Boccioni, Max Ernst, Francis Picabia and Marcel Duchamp, while production from the grey zone between art and engineering included items as diverse as Leonardo's drawings for flying apparatuses, Lyonel Feininger's toy prototypes for miniature locomotives, Christopher Polhem's *Letters from Mechanical Alphabet*, and cartoons from the 19th and 20th centuries (Winsor McCay, Rube Goldberg and others). Contemporary art production was represented by variations on Pop Art and Hyperrealism (such as James Rosenquist and Claes Oldenburg), Nouveau Réalisme (César) and kinetic sculpture (Jean Tinguely, Takis, Hans Haacke), while Nam June Paik and the duo Marian Zazeela and La Monte Young represented post-Fluxus experimentation.

In his catalogue essay Hultén dramatises the machine as a Janus-faced trope that encompasses both human ingenuity and folly.[8] Novelists and wayward thinkers ranging from Mary Shelley and Samuel Butler to Julien Offroy de La Mettrie and Jules Verne offered unexpected, literary perspectives, while quotes from Marx and social historians allowed Hultén to flesh out the social dimension of the exhibition theme. In his *Art Bulletin* review of *The Machine*, William A. Camfield emphasises Hultén's "social commentary" à propos of the photograph *Nigeria* (1960) by Ed van der Elsken that depicts "a Nigerian tending an awesome, antiquated apparatus" (as Camfield writes): in his caption to the photograph Hultén notes that "the mechanical age seems linked to the age of colonialism ... both were based on the instinct for exploitation" and Camfield comments that such "moving and illuminating ... remarks are hardly the standard fare of scholarly, historical exhibitions."[9]

Such perspectives can be said to modify the Eurocentrism of *The Machine*, as did its inclusion of Russian constructivism at a time when the recovery of the historical avant-gardes was still tainted by the Cold War. The anti-communist Documenta, for instance, made no concessions to Eastern European avant-gardes before its sixth iteration in 1977; and a few months before the opening of *The Machine*, Documenta 4 in 1968 was nicknamed "Documenta Americana" for its preponderance of British and North American Pop artists. By contrast, at Moderna Museet earlier that same year, Hultén had presented the first exhibition outside of Russia on the work of Vladimir Tatlin. Tatlin was also a key player in Hultén's art-and-engineering genealogy in *The Machine*, where the copy of Tatlin's model for his *Monument to the Third International* (1919–20), built in 1968 by Ulf Linde and Per Olof Ultvedt for the Moderna Museet exhibition, graced MoMA's sculpture garden.

Similar to other curatorial efforts on art and technology in the years to come, such as Los Angeles County Museum of Art's (LACMA) Art and Technology Program (1967–71), gender was a non-issue made invisible in a patriarchal framework.[10] Implicitly, and therefore essentially, technology was a male domain: if *The Machine* feminised machines such as racing cars, technologies of gendered reproductive labour were absent. In Hultén's dramatisation of a Hegelian struggle between human and machine about servitude and mastery, kitchen machines would probably have connoted a domestic domain out of step with the exhibition's heroic narrative. It seems relevant to raise the point, though, seeing how the televised "Kitchen Debate" between Soviet President Nikita Khrushchev and American Vice President Richard Nixon in 1959 had made the kitchen a battleground of bloc techno-politics. Besides, a gender sensitive perspective might have introduced other hermeneutical vectors on the machine than the projectile ones of speed and vision.

The exhibition's retrospective character was counterintuitive for announcing a new era and instead engaging with the one that had passed. As Öyvind Fahlström wrote in his review of the show for *Dagens Nyheter*: "If you wanted to allude to technology's accelerating reformation of the world … you would probably point primarily to the computer and what it achieves, automation, thinking machines, robots. Military technology and space technology and their art-like uselessness and singular focus on quality."[11] On the note of accelerationism, Hultén's subtitle "the end of the mechanical age" not only echoes Benjamin but also Marshall McLuhan's epochal claims of the end of the "Gutenberg Galaxy" – the modern

From the exhibition *The Machine*,
The Museum of Modern Art, New York, 1968

world of the printed word, a hypothesis that he popularised in his seminal anti-book *The Medium is the Massage*, from 1967.[12] It is hard to imagine that Hultén was unaware of McLuhan's very influential and popular writing, and you might get the impression that he took McLuhan fleetingly into account, while ultimately being unwilling – or simply omitting – to integrate his thinking.

McLuhan displaced mechanical apparatus to communicative ambience, and employed his expanded, performative notion of media – "all media work us over completely" – to claim that "any understanding of social and cultural change is impossible without a knowledge of the way media work as environments."[13] We can speculate that McLuhan's privileged terms of media and ambience would have complicated the homology mechanical apparatus/art object that organised the curatorial syntax of *The Machine* and its social and aesthetic commentary. Hultén's focus on the machine also distanced him from another dominant take on technology at the time – namely, the way Martin Heidegger in his post-war writing was concerned with the metaphysical essence of technology as a rationale and an attitude towards the world.[14]

McLuhan took issue with the linearity of progress with his famous notion of a tribal "global village" as a "simultaneous happening" in which "electric circularity has overthrown the regime of 'time' and 'space'".[15] For Hultén, on the other hand, progress was (still) a matter of a sort of race against technology in which art played an essential role in humanizing the former. But the split that had caused destructive progress could be healed in an integration of art with (other) forms of *tekhné* in an aesthetic wholeness of knowledges and practices – and hence of society – that according to Hultén had existed in ancient Greece prior to disciplinarity. Thus, to Hultén, in ancient Greece "there was no more opposition between nature and the application of natural laws in technics than there was between technics and art".[16] This imagined reunification had the added purpose of removing art from its pedestal where it has been "respectfully venerated, and consequently quite misunderstood" in the abandonment of "the humanist standpoint [in favour of] a sophistical defence of property".[17] Thus Hultén argues:

> Clearly, if we believe in either life or art, we must assume complete [human] domination over machines, to subject them to our will, and direct them so that they may serve life in the most efficient way

– taking as our criterion the totality of human life on this planet.

In planning for such a world, and in helping to bring it into being, artists are more important than politicians, and even than technicians. But, of course, it is not artists in whom we ordinarily most place our confidence.[18]

Hultén also cites overproduction and industrialisation's "reckless exploitation of the earth's natural resources".[19] Not only the period vocabulary in which "nature" is seen as a question of resources, and not as a planetary life support system, but also Hultén's rearranging of signifiers of art, nature, and technology in favour of a new naturalness or transparency of art and technology, reveal why nature disappears in *The Machine*. Today we have the theoretical tools to call out such an anthropo- and logocentrism that erases nature in the sublation of art and technology under enlightened human agency – a rationalising impulse crowned by Hultén's techno-optimism in which artists are needed to keep history from being rudderless: an attempt at bending the storm of progress to morality through art, as it were. As Amelia Jones notes, the connection between art and humanism is a complacent one.[20] In Hultén's case, this complacency comes down to his conviction about the separability between human and machine that issues the promise that modernity can have it both ways: a world of harmonious technological efficiency *and* aesthetic presence.

From another point of view, nature as a blind spot in *The Machine* is reflected in John Canaday's *New York Times* review of the exhibition.[21] In the show's juxtaposition between art and machine, the machine betters art: in this way Canaday suggests that no modern painting or sculpture can compete in beauty with the machines that inspired artists to either revolt against them or to unite with them (a view that resonates in the "machine-age formalism" propagated by, for instance, Fernand Léger and his claim that the machine had an inherent beauty because of its lack of aesthetic intentionality).[22] One implication of how art can be beaten at its own game by the machine is that the human-made replaces nature as the aesthetic ground and measure of that which within a traditional aesthetic is to be imitated – a recipe (Hultén's intentions to the contrary) for the conceptual obliteration of nature.

This rhetoric is familiar from Experiments in Art and Technology (E.A.T.), the New York-based non-profit organisation founded

cc: Pontus Hultén ✓
Miss Dudley

February 28, 1968

Mr. Frederick S. Wight
Director
The Art Galleries
University of California
at Los Angeles
405 Hilgard Avenue
Los Angeles, California 90024

Dear Mr. Wight:

For a major exhibition we are preparing called THE MACHINE we are trying to track a painting by Charles Sheeler, Suspended Power, 1939. I see from the catalogue that you included this work in an exhibition of Sheeler's work in 1954 and at that time it was in the collection of the S. Morgan Smith Company, York, Pennsylvania. We have tried to get in touch with this company but they no longer seem to be in existence, and I wonder if you could give me any more information or if you have any knowledge of the present whereabouts of the painting. It is a matter of some urgency for us to find the picture and I should be most grateful if you could reply to this letter at the earliest opportunity.

With thanks for any help you are able to give us,

Yours sincerely,

Jennifer Licht
Assistant Curator

this show is doomed

!

Letter from the assistant curator Jennifer Licht to Frederick S. Wight, director of the Art Galleries, University of California

in 1966 by engineers Billy Klüver and Fred Waldhauer with artists Robert Rauschenberg and Robert Whitman. The pre-eminent art-technology initiative in the United States at the time, E.A.T. was created with the agenda to promote collaborations between artists and engineers outside of the art museums and the art market.[23] A section of *The Machine* included eight new commissions as the result of a competition "for engineers and artists" organised between MoMA and E.A.T. (simultaneously with *The Machine*, 150 works submitted to the E.A.T. competition were shown at the Brooklyn Museum under the title *Some More Beginnings* and the direction of Klüver). Hultén's close connection with E.A.T. president Klüver was a significant "New York connection" and the organisation was included in the exhibitions *Utopia and Visions 1871–1981* (1971) and *New York Collection for Stockholm* (1973) during Moderna Museet's formative years.[24] The section of the exhibition co-organised with E.A.T., though, remained something of a sideshow to the main event at MoMA. Reviews reveal scant interest in it, and the only digital work in *The Machine* – to be found in the E.A.T. section – was characterised by Öyvind Fahlström as "naive".[25] If *The Machine* pulled its punches in relation to the cybernetic age to follow the end of the mechanical one, that same autumn curator Jasia Reichardt opened *Cybernetic Serendipity* at London's Institute of Contemporary Arts, an exhibition that differed markedly from *The Machine* by putting artistic speculation with thinking machines centre stage.[26]

E.A.T.'s vision for the artist-engineer alliance resonates in a tendency among avant-garde artists during the New York Dada period to privilege the engineer over the artist. As Amelia Jones notes, Duchamp, the anti-art genius, "liked to proclaim that he considered himself an engineer rather than an artist".[27] Hultén's inclusion of cars and other machines can be called a Duchampian curatorial gesture, yet devoid of Dada's exposure of "the absurdity" of distinctions between industrial and aesthetic. Jones again:

> The avant-garde's valuation of the engineer or everyday worker also functioned to privilege the untutored eye, which intuited a kind of machine-age beauty that overtrained artists could no longer see (the "freshness" attributed to the engineer's or laborer's eye is thus akin to the freshness of the so-called primitive, who is not overschooled in bourgeois habits and thus supposedly has a purer, less adulterated capacity to appreciate true beauty).[28]

If *The Machine*, with works by Duchamp, Picabia and even Elsa Freytag von Loringhoven, can be seen as a curatorial response to the modern experience of the threatening aspects of urban industrialism and the social changes that accompanied it, the exhibition also came, via E.A.T., with a specific proposal for how to overcome estrangement and trauma through a marriage of artmaking and instrumental reason – an aesthetic functionalism, to call it that, that contrasts with the machine works of New York Dada as "extremely complex [and] incomplete negotiations of the violent challenges to the masculine subject in urban industrialism."[29] That is, if echoes persisted from New York Dada in *The Machine*, Hultén now employed its ethos of techno-primitivism to rather different ends.

"A deeply personal exhibition" – The curatorial subject

The Machine was very positively, if also somewhat politely received. *The Village Voice*'s John Perrault noted circuitously that "the still tentative marriage between art and technology ... offers the possibility of the reasonable exploitation of intuition and the intuitional exploitation of reason."[30] You don't get the feeling that the show hit a raw nerve, the way *Movement in Art* was "upsetting, depressing and immoral" as *Svenska Dagbladet* summarised *The Machine*'s predecessor at Moderna Museet.[31]

The conservative lining on *The Machine* seeped into its social context. Thus, before *The Village Voice* reviewed the show, Blaire Sabol had covered its opening in the paper's fashion column. Here a photograph shows art critic Jill Johnston in "Houston original cowboy outfit in pastel brocade", while Factory star Ultra Violet "remained violently velveted as usual". Such sartorial aplomb stood out, though, as the "black tie invite brought ... the middle-aged man's return to normalcy" after the Summer of Love's exotic inspirations. On the side of women's fashion, too, it was a *retour à l'ordre* against bohemian excess: "there was no question that there was more bulk, hard steel and wire in the female display than in the machines, due to Seventh Avenue's bust-binding ideas".[32]

One of the big social events of *The Machine* was Hultén himself, whose persona graced the show in the manner of a great conductor or film director. Understandably, Swedish media were agog over the Moderna Museet director's guest appearance at MoMA, the most prestigious art institution in the Western World at the time.

Above: Pontus Hultén in the exhibition *The Machine*, New York, 1968.
Below: Marcel Duchamp, *The Large Glass* (1915–1923/1961) from the Moderna Museet collection in the same exhibition, 1968

Swedish journalists covered the exhibition as an unfolding event and followed Hultén around town, from a glamorous reception in his honour at the Consulate General of Sweden, with Andy Warhol, Robert Rauschenberg and other art world luminaries in attendance, to reports about the American reception of the show, including a walk-through of the exhibition and interview with its maker by Fahlström (again!) for the Swedish national broadcaster.[33] Also MoMA's *Members Newsletter* emphasised that "the character of the exhibition … derives from the personality of the man who organized it".[34] Archival photographs illustrate the point: a casually dressed Hultén appears to have moved his office, or at least the telephone, into the galleries of MoMA, where he is also seen to be engaged in hands-on installation of works. There is even a media buzz that he is in line for "the powerful post of director of museum collections, a job now held by the distinguished Alfred Barr".[35]

Written by Hultén, and with its colourful and wonderfully clunky metal cover design by Anders Österlin, the exhibition catalogue was an important part of *The Machine*. In June 1971 – more than two years after the opening of *The Machine*, and well after the tour was over – the catalogue was "the primary object" of William A. Camfield's *Art Bulletin* review of *The Machine*.[36] Here he dwells on the cover in "thin sheet metal, embossed with a scrawling script title, *The Machine*, and with a prosaic, polychrome design based on a photograph of the façade of the Museum of Modern Art".[37] With its air of a graphic novel or some sort of elegantly canned book, the cover evokes the industrial origins of Pop Art's visuality. An object of the mechanical age that conveys an image of the technological city's exhibitionary apparatus, the catalogue makes for a premonition of the Centre Pompidou, the museum of which Hultén would become founding director (1973–81) a few years later.

The critical afterlife of *The Machine* takes Hultén's project into the 1970s, where it can be compared with another modernist end game: Harald Szeemann's exhibition *Junggesellenmaschinen/Les machines célibataires* (Bachelor Machines), which toured to no less than nine West European venues between 1975 to 1977, including Malmö Konsthall in Sweden, where it was shown in the autumn of 1976. Like *The Machine*, *Les machines célibataires* was historically anchored, according to Szeemann precisely to the era between 1850 and 1925, and also awarded a central role to Duchamp.[38] Additionally, a personally voiced écriture was important to both "curauteurs" as we might call them: Szeemann's endeavour, too, can be called "a deeply personal exhibition" as Fahlström characterised *The Machine*.[39]

However, if *The Machine*'s art history was trained on techno-humanism, Szeemann's show put desire over morality in no uncertain terms, bypassing the earnestness of the art and technology theme and instead focusing on the angst-ridden limits and perverse supplements of a mechanised modernity. Intellectually adventurous, Szeemann's proposition provided a post-Freudian exegesis of the machine as a modern myth of obsession and sublimation with a roster of contemporary thinkers, including Michel de Certeau, Jean-François Lyotard and Michel Serres, who accompanied the viewer to roam the garden paths of artistic idiosyncrasy and post-structuralist critiques of modernity.[40] Hultén and Szeemann quote the same passage from Michel Carrouges's Duchamp study *Les Machines célibataires* (1954) for their respective catalogue texts, however it was clearly Szeemann who made the most of Carrouges's diagnosis of the bachelor machine as an "a fantastic image that transforms love into a mechanics of death".[41] If Hultén's announcement of the end of the mechanical age hinged on his tactful loyalty to "the humanist standpoint", Szeemann explicitly set the libidinal economy of his bachelor machines to work on the doomed metaphysics of the modern era.[42] Amplifying his curatorial concept of "individual mythologies" from Documenta 5 in 1972, Szeemann insisted that his exhibition theme was premised on its being an "eminently political … mythology" including his own role in its work on historical limits: "The exhibition organiser … chooses an epoch that has to be overcome for there to be a continuation (for him? For others as well?)".[43] Allegedly capable of being at once individualistic, mytho-visualising and political, Szeemann's exhibition was no doubt as excessive, self-centred and otherwise repressive as the Western modernity he undertook to deconstruct. It might be said that his raw and experimental curatorial stance didn't commit the institutional sin of taming the avant-garde. It did, however, flagrantly turn woman into its historical casualty. As Caroline Jones writes: "Crucial to the ideology of the bachelor machine was the existential fiction of its autonomy as a male generator of forms and activities (no females reproducing here)."[44]

With certain telling overlaps and very different aims and methods, Hultén and Szeemann searched for an exit from the modern era through the encounter between art and machine. Szeemann

Jean Tinguely, *Méta-Matic No 17* (1959) from the Moderna Museet collection, in the exhibition *The Machine,* The Museum of Modern Art, New York, 1968

managed to penetrate (priapic pun intended) an opening between eras and *épistémès* by interrupting positivistic and ameliorative ideas of technology, but his exhibition was a dark and decadent option rather than a promise for the future. As for *The Machine*, Hultén's show was also attuned to the historical avant-garde's play with machinic imaginary, yet devoid of irony and ultimately blocking the passage out of the modern with modernistic promises issued by its humanistic *Weltanschauung*.

In his "Theses on the Philosophy of History" Walter Benjamin mentions the unbeatable, mechanical chess-playing Turk, a sham automaton at the 18th-century Viennese court whose alleged perfection was ultimately owed to the fact that someone operated it from the inside. In Benjamin's famous analogy, Marxism could only explain history if it, like the chess-robot impostor, draws upon hidden powers – in the case of dialectical materialism, those of theology. Maybe Hultén's exhibition had a ghost in its inner workings, too, by investing art with a similar theological affordance. The exhibition's vision could only be redeemed by the appearance of some metaphysical entity that is external to history – a "messianic time", to use Benjamin's concept, or the aesthetic means with which a meaningful union of art and technology could be restored in Hultén's *grand récit*.[45]

Postscript

Today it takes a leap of the imagination to think of "art" and "technology" as separate entities. It was with this in mind that I curated the group show *Mud Muses – A Rant About Technology* at Moderna Museet in 2019–20. The exhibition proposed that the (historyladen, if not downright anachronistic) art and technology formula in a deliberately untimely fashion might be relevant for analysing technology as a "realized condition" in the present.[46] As I wrote, the exhibition encompassed:

> a longer timespan than that defined by the rise of the Internet and the present hegemony of digital mediation … providing the opportunity to assess historical change and to consider directions that will shape our future.[47]

The exhibition owed its title to Robert Rauschenberg's eccentric installation *Mud Muse* (1968–71) and science-fiction writer Ursula

K. Le Guin's 2004 essay "A Rant About 'Technology'". Rauschenberg's work (NMSK 2174) in the Moderna Museet collection consists of a large, minimalist vat of glass and steel, in which plopping sounds, created by compressed air, pass through valves at its bottom to make little geysers erupt in thousands of pounds of synthetic mud made from a recipe of glycerin and finely ground volcanic ash. Through the LACMA's Art and Technology Program, Rauschenberg collaborated with personnel from the industrial conglomerate Teledyne Inc., an aerospace-oriented industry with commercial and military clients. It was Teledyne that, in 1973, donated the work through E.A.T. to Moderna Museet, where it arrived in a group of other North American acquisitions and donations. The project was negatively received by some local artists and activists with accusations of "technocratic emptiness", cultural imperialism and symbolic endorsement of the US military-industrial complex at the height of the Vietnam War.[48]

"Technology is the active human interface with the material world", according to Le Guin's definition of technology that is not only more value-neutral and non-deterministic than many, but also anthropocentric, and very broad.[49] With this, Le Guin takes the concept beyond objects of substance – machines such as "a computer or a jet bomber" – and undoes its providential essence of being always and only modern. Instead, as an object for sci-fi thinking, technology is uprooted from the rationality of the present and rendered movable in historical times and spaces.

Through contributions from, among others, Mumbai's Vision Exchange Workshop (1969–74) and the contemporary Johannesburg collective CUSS Group, *Mud Muses* set out to challenge "the geopolitics of a North Atlantic axis that has dominated histories of technology and art – including some of those told at Moderna Museet" (to quote myself again).[50] Philosopher Yuk Hui's postcolonial analysis of cosmotechnics engaged with, among other contributions, cosmograms by the Amerindian shamans Armando, Paulino and Antônio Marubo, while a feminist perspective took aim at "undaddying" the techno-patriarchy.[51] Thus in an attempt to eschew boosterism and techno-fix ideologies, the exhibition invited a range of artistic approaches from the last half-century to explore – or even explode – the concept of technology with a multitude of concerns, from the vantage point of a 21st-century art institution expected to perform in a digitised experience economy.

Today the question of technology has an almost ontological character, both from the point of view of how human life is technologically circumscribed and fundamentally enframed, and from the perspective of artificial intelligence that is in the process of making tech cognizant and sentient. Through its efforts towards "undaddying" and decolonising technology, *Mud Muses* was critically tied to the legacy of Hultén and the art-and-technology framework of the 1960s – with hindsight, the exhibition prepared the ground for a rupture with the modern through its effort towards building historical accountability for the concept of technology, but its legacy-oriented starting point arguably prevented it from putting the Western world's angel of history to rest, or at least turning its head in the right direction.

At a point when life itself on this planet is under threat, thus revealing the naïveté and anthropocentric limitations of Hultén's vision of an *Aufhebung* of art and technology, a critical radicalisation – or *exacerbation* – of the premise of techno-ontology is called for. If technology is the fulcrum around which human culture reproduces itself as such, then what would happen if the nature/culture binary is flipped in favour of nature? In other words, what would be a post-cultural concept of technology? As Karen Barad suggests, "What if we were to understand culture as something nature does?"[52] A reworking of the human/non-human and the nature/culture binaries (that also takes into account that nature is a "projection" and a "materialized fantasy" as Donna Haraway puts it) might free up a necessary critical and creative space for a contemporary interrogation of technology.[53]

As for Hultén, his institutional thinking around the art-technology nexus was more radical than his curatorial work on *The Machine*. As Kim West points out, cybernetics was part and parcel of his and Moderna Museet's attempt to reconfigure the exhibitionary apparatus itself.[54] When plans were made during the mid-1960s for Moderna Museet to be moved from its then (and present) location at Skeppsholmen to central Stockholm, Hultén and curator Pär Stolpe reimagined the modern museum of art as a blend between Tatlin's tower and a sophisticated databank and transmission station. Hultén and Stolpe drew a concentric diagram that undid the isolationism of the modernist white cube, instead outlining the museum as a spherical institution. The outermost sphere "connects to the universe of everyday life, characterized by an accelerated concentration of information"; the second sphere represents workshops in which the "means of production are available" for museum-goers; the third layer is home to presentations of the workshop productions in "different manifestations: visual arts, films, photo, dance, concerts".[55] The core of the diagram, finally, is reserved for the memory of the processed information, the museum's collection. Such a Moderna Museet would never be realised in Stockholm, but with Hultén's appointment at the Centre Pompidou, his and Stolpe's vision of an artificial mind or architectural machine opening up to the flows of the social field came closer to seeing the light of day, *mutatis mutandis*. But this is yet another point where the history of Hultén's *The Machine as Seen at the End of the Mechanical Age* forks out into a different future.

1. Press release no. 123 for *The Machine,* 25 November, 1968. https://www.moma.org/calendar/exhibitions/2776 (23 August, 2022). The exhibition was on until 9 February, 1969.

2. In 1965 d'Harnoncourt asked Hultén whether he "should like to organize an exhibition on kinetic art" and this also implies that *The Machine* was developed for a US context. See K. G. Pontus Hultén, "Foreword and Acknowledgments", *The Machine as Seen at the End of the Mechanical Age* (exh. cat.), ed. K. G. Pontus Hultén, New York: The Museum of Modern Art, 1968, p. 3.

3. K. G. Pontus Hultén, *The Machine as Seen at the End of the Mechanical Age*, 1968, p. 3.

4. Walter Benjamin, "Theses on the Philosophy of History", *Illuminations. Essays and Reflections*, ed. Hannah Arendt, London: Penguin Random House, 1955/2015, pp. 245–256.

5. Exhibitions, The Machine 1–7. MMA PHA 4.2.52–58.

6. K. G. Pontus Hultén, *The Machine as Seen at the End of the Mechanical Age*, 1968, p. 3.

7. Hand-written comment on copy of letter, regarding a request for help with locating "a painting by Charles Sheeler, Suspended Power, 1939". Letter from Jennifer Licht to Frederick S. Wight, Director of The Art Galleries, University of California, 28 February, 1968. MMA PHA 4.2.55.

8. K. G. Pontus Hultén, "Introduction", *The Machine as Seen at the End of the Mechanical Age* (exh. cat.), ed. K. G. Pontus Hultén, 1968, pp. 6–13.

9. William A. Camfield, review of *The Machine as Seen at the End of the Mechanical Age*, *The Art Bulletin*, vol. 53, issue 2, 1971, pp. 275–277. K. G. Pontus Hultén, *The Machine as Seen at the End of the Mechanical Age*, 1968, p. 175. Scholars such as Susan Buck-Morss have later agreed with this perspective, but rather from the inverse perspective of colonialism being a precondition for the mechanical age: "It is significant that all of this [the Haitian Revolution in 1791 and its repercussions in Europe] happened before the introduction of machine labor on a grand scale. By imagining modernity as synonymous with Europe, we have misunderstood how much modern capitalism was a product of the colonial system, which was in many ways ahead of European developments." See Susan Buck-Morss, *Hegel, Haiti, and Universal History*, Pittsburgh: University of Pittsburgh Press, 2009, p. 100.

10. LACMA's A&T Program, as it was nicknamed, included not a single woman on its list of sixty-three male artists.

11. Öyvind Fahlström, "En lustfylld maskindans", *Dagens Nyheter* (Stockholm), 4 January, 1969. Fahlström also reviewed *Rörelsen i konsten* (Movement in Art), endorsing it as an exhibition that has "the nature of factory, nursery, laboratory, madhouse, greenhouse, fairground; anything but a museum." Öyvind Fahlström, "Rörelsen i konsten – en förstummande upplevelse", *Expressen* (Stockholm), 19 May, 1961.

12. Similarly, Norbert Wiener is quoted in Hultén's catalogue essay, yet as Fahlström also notes, cybernetics – neither as a theory of systems, nor in terms of thinking machines – is not employed in *The Machine* beyond

being checked as a marker of contemporaneity. See Öyvind Fahlström, "En lustfylld maskindans", *Dagens Nyheter*, 4 January, 1969.

13. Marshall McLuhan and Quentin Fiore, *The Medium Is the Massage. An Inventory of Effects*, New York: Simon & Schuster, 1967, p. 26.

14. Closer both to New York City and the field of art, *The Machine* also took a different trajectory than the MIT's pioneering interdisciplinary art programme at the Center for Advanced Visual Studies, founded in 1967 by the artist György Kepes, for whom the meeting with technology played out on "art's civic scale" in the entanglement between urban and environmental milieus. See György Kepes, "Toward Civic Art", *Leonardo*, vol. 4, no. 1, 1971, pp. 69–73.

15. Marshall McLuhan and Quentin Fiore, *The Medium Is the Massage. An Inventory of Effects*, 1967, pp. 16 and 63.

16. Pontus Hultén, "Introduction", *The Machine as Seen at the End of the Mechanical Age*, 1968, p. 10.

17. Ibid.

18. Ibid., p. 11.

19. Ibid., p. 10.

20. Amelia Jones, *Irrational Modernism. A Neurasthenic History of New York Dada*, Cambridge, MA: The MIT Press, 2004.

21. John Canaday, "Art. Machines Fascinate", *New York Times*, 28 November, 1968.

22. Amelia Jones, *Irrational Modernism. A Neurasthenic History of New York Dada*, 2004, p. 139.

23. The art historical authority of initiatives associated with E.A.T. is being renegotiated by critical readings such as Kim West's when he juxtaposes the "oligarchic" ethos of E.A.T.'s Automation House with Hultén's outline for a new Moderna Museet and its "radically democratic" vision derived partly from the Swedish post-war welfare state, partly from a Russian constructivist tradition. See Kim West, "Mud Muse, Mutatis Mutandis: Notes on Two Models of the Art-Technology Alliance", *Mud Muses. A Rant About Technology*, ed. Lars Bang Larsen, Moderna Museet exhibition catalogue no. 407, Stockholm: Moderna Museet, 2019, pp. 71–87.

24. See Pontus Hultén, "The New York Connection", *Teknologi för livet: Om Experiments in Art and Technology*, Paris: Schultz Förlag AB and Norrköping: Norrköpings Konstmuseum, 2004, pp. 143–147. Originally published in *Moderna Museet 1958–1983*, eds. Olle Granath and Monica Nieckels, Stockholm: Moderna Museet, 1983, pp. 54–57. For an interview with Billy Klüver see Marianne Hultman, "Our Man in New York. An Interview with Billy Klüver on his Collaboration with Moderna Museet", *The History Book. On Moderna Museet 1958–2008*, eds. Anna Tellgren and Martin Sundberg, Stockholm: Moderna Museet and Göttingen: Steidl, 2008, pp. 233–256.

25. Öyvind Fahlström, "En lustfylld maskindans", *Dagens Nyheter*, 4 January, 1969. The work in question was *Studies in Perception I* (1968), a computer-processed photographic print of a female nude submitted to the competition by Leon D. Harmon and Kenneth C. Knowlton.

26. The press release for *Cybernetic Serendipity* from 1 June, 1968, is to be found in the archive of *The Machine*, indicating that Hultén was aware of the London exhibition. The release, that includes a list of biweekly "Cybernetic Serendipity Lectures" describes the exhibition as including: "1. Computer generated graphics, computer animated film, computer composed and played music, computer verse and texts"; "2. Cybernetic devices as works of art, remote control robots, Cybernetic environments, and painting machines"; and "3. Demonstrations of how computers work, the history of Cybernetics, and daily film shows between 12–2 pm". MMA PHA 4.2.55.

27. Amelia Jones, *Irrational Modernism. A Neurasthenic History of New York Dada*, 2004, p. 46.

28. Ibid., pp. 137–139.

29. Ibid., p. 125.

30. John Perrault, "art to make it new" [sic!], *The Village Voice*, 15 December, 1968.

31. Catharina Bauer, "Konstnären och maskinen", *Svenska Dagbladet* (Stockholm), 15 December, 1968.

32. Blaire Sabol, "Fashion Column", *The Village Voice*, 5 December, 1968.

33. A *Svenska Dagbladet* report on 1 December, 1968, refers to the reception at the Consulate General of Sweden in New York; *Dagens Nyheter*, 6 December, 1968, mentions Fahlström's interview with Hultén.

34. Helen M. Franc, "The Machine as Seen at the End of the Mechanical Age", *Members Newsletter*, New York: The Museum of Modern Art, November–December, 1968.

35. See "Papa for MOMA", *New York Times*, 8 January, 1968 (probably written by Grace Glueck).

36. William A. Camfield, review of *The Machine as Seen at the End of the Mechanical Age*, *The Art Bulletin*, vol. 53, issue 2, 1971, pp. 275–277. The rest of the publication's design is credited to Hultén, Gösta Svensson and Anders Österlin's collaborator, John Melin; the cover photograph was taken by MoMA curator Alicia Legg. Österlin and Melin created the catalogues for the *She – A Cathedrral* and Andy Warhol exhibitions at Moderna Museet, among other graphic materials for the museum.

37. Ibid. Delightfully nerdy reviews of the catalogue were also published in professional journals for graphic designers, for instance in *Grafisk Faktorstidning* (Grafiska faktors- och tjänstemannaförbundet, Stockholm), no. 5, 1969, p. 66.

38. Where Szeemann quoted Duchamp's *The Large Glass* for his title, Hultén also gave Duchamp a strong showing in *The Machine* with seven works, including Ulf Linde's replica of *The Large Glass* (1915–23/1961) from the Moderna Museet collection, and *Nude Descending a Staircase* numbers 1 (1911) and 3 (1916) from the collections at the Philadelphia Museum of Art.

39. Öyvind Fahlström, "En lustfylld maskindans", *Dagens Nyheter*, 4 January, 1969.

40. It can be added that in the line-up of contributors to Szeemann's catalogue, Gilles Deleuze and Félix Guattari's schizo-analysis of their 1972 *Anti-Oedipus*, where they elaborate the idea of the subconscious as a machine from a Freudo-Marxist point of view, is conspicuously absent. Also in the case of Szeemann's show, the exhibition catalogue plays a discursive role beyond that of documentation and interpretive aid. And Szeemann must have been aware of *The Machine*: a reproduction of Max Ernst's *Petite machine construite par lui-même…* (1919) on page 127 in the exhibition catalogue of *Junggesellenmaschinen /Les machines célibataires* (1975) is taken from the catalogue (p. 121) of Hultén's show. For interesting installation views from various touring venues of *Les machines célibataires*, see *Harald Szeemann. With by Through Because Towards Despite. Catalogue of All Exhibitions 1957–2005*, eds. Tobia Bezzola and Roman Kurzmeyer, Zürich: Edition Voldemeer and Vienna: Springer Verlag, 2007, pp. 392–405.

41. Michel Carrouges, "Mode d'emploi", *Junggesellenmaschinen/Les machines célibataires* (exh. cat.), eds. Harald Szeemann and Jean Clair, Venice: Alfieri, 1975, pp. 21–49. The passage by Carrouges quoted by both Hultén and Szeemann reads: "It would be childish to believe that the greatest geniuses of our time have amused themselves with illusory games and have wilfully disguised their thought. However bizarre their great games may seem, they have made apparent in fiery characters the major myth in which is written the fourfold tragedy of our age: the Gordian knot of the clash among mechanization, terror, eroticism, and religion or anti-religion. These are the portentous alarm signals that they are sending out to us, from the heights of their observatories erected atop high towers, at the heart of the modern tempest." See Pontus Hultén, *The Machine as Seen at the End of the Mechanical Age*, 1968, p. 6, and Harald Szeemann, *Junggesellenmaschinen/ Les machines célibataires*, 1975, p. 7.

42. Pontus Hultén, *The Machine as Seen at the End of the Mechanical Age*, 1968, p. 10.

43. Harald Szeemann, *Junggesellenmaschinen/Les machines célibataires*, 1975, pp. 9 and 10.

44. Caroline A. Jones, *The Global Work of Art. World's Fairs, Biennials, and the Aesthetics of Experience*, Chicago: The University of Chicago Press, 2017, p. 190. The sexism of *Les machines célibataires* didn't pass unnoticed upon its showing at Malmö Konsthall. On its front page, "Malmös fria kulturtidning" (Malmö's free cultural newspaper) *Den Hialöse* pronounced it "lecherous" (essentially, an old man's exhibition) and condemned what was understood to be its excessive strain on the Konsthall's municipal budget. See *Den Hialöse* (Malmö), October, 1976, unpaginated.

45. Walter Benjamin, "Theses on the Philosophy of History", *Illuminations. Essays and Reflections*, ed. Hannah Arendt, London: Penguin Random House, 1955/2015, pp. 245–256.

46. Lars Bang Larsen, "A Map of the Show: Coordinates in Time, Space, and Ideas", *Mud Muses. A Rant About Technology*, ed. Lars Bang Larsen,

Moderna Museet exhibition catalogue no. 407, Stockholm: Moderna Museet, 2019, p. 40.

47. Ibid.

48. See Marianne Hultman, "New York Collection for Stockholm", *Teknologi för livet. Om Experiments in Art and Technology*, 2004, pp. 160–171, and *New York Collection for Stockholm*, ed. Björn Springfeldt, Moderna Museet exhibition catalogue no. 111, Stockholm: Moderna Museet, 1973. See also *The New York Collection for Stockholm: Final Report*, 12 August, 1974. MMA MA F1a:68.

49. Ursula K. Le Guin, "A Rant About 'Technology'", *Mud Muses. A Rant About Technology*, 2019, p. 24.

50. Lars Bang Larsen, "A Map of the Show: Coordinates in Time, Space, and Ideas", *Mud Muses. A Rant About Technology*, 2019, p. 42.

51. Soda_Jerk's video *Undaddy Mainframe* (2014) is their tribute to fellow Australian outfit VNS Matrix who coined the term *cyberfeminist* in their *Cyberfeminist Manifesto for the 21st Century* (1991). Other artists and collectives in the exhibition included: Ian Cheng, Vision Exchange Workshop with Nalini Malani and Akbar Padamsee, Branko Petrović, CUSS Group, Primer, Sidsel Meineche Hansen and Cultural Capital Cooperative, Charlotte Johannesson, Anna Lundh, The Otolith Group, Suzanne Treister, Lucy Siyao Liu, Nomeda and Gediminas Urbonas, Anna Sjödahl, and Jenna Sutela, alongside Kooperative für Darstellungspolitik (exhibition architecture) and VARV VARV (graphic design).

52. Karen Barad, "Nature's Queer Performativity", *Kvinder, køn & forskning*, no. 1–2, 2012, pp. 25–53.

53. Donna J. Haraway, *Modest_Witness@Second_Millennium.FemaleMan©_Meets_OncoMouse™. Feminism and Technoscience*, New York: Routledge, 1997, p. 34.

54. Kim West, *The Exhibitionary Complex. Exhibition, Apparatus, and Media from Kulturhuset to the Centre Pompidou, 1963–1977* (diss.), Södertörn Studies in Art History and Aesthetics 4, Huddinge: Södertörn University, 2017.

55. Ibid., p. 10. Quoted from Yann Pavie, "Vers le musée du futur. Entretien avec Pontus Hultén", *Opus International*, no. 24–25, 1971, pp. 56–65. Translated from French to English by Kim West.

PONTUS HULTÉN'S COLLECTION OF BOOKS

Marcel Duchamp. Catalogue Raisonné, ed. Jean Clair, Paris: Musée National d'Art Moderne, Centre Georges Pompidou, 1977

Pontus Hultén's Collection of Books. Books as Art and Art in Book Format

Annika Gunnarsson

Pontus Hultén presented himself as being free and radical in interviews and conversations. His honed understanding of contemporary society and new developments in art is also well documented, but the fact that he was also a traditionalist is not highlighted as frequently. Hulten's library is an example of the latter quality. It reveals his social position and academic background. With his library, Hultén joins the ranks of illustrious people who have collected books as signs of erudition and influence.[1] As a means of keeping up with international events, and to build their own knowledge, these people simply collected printed material. Some would claim that Hultén manifested his legitimacy as a museum director by donating his archives, his books and his art collection to Moderna Museet, and thereby having a room dedicated to him, the Pontus Hultén Study Gallery.[2]

Pontus Hultén also followed the beaten track by participating in designing the catalogues that accompanied the exhibitions he produced.[3] The catalogues, he said, should be visual and tactile in addition to their educational and informative content.[4] With regard to the former, he adopted contemporary ideas of the book as a medium for performative purposes, as demonstrated also by his own book about Jean Tinguely from 1972.[5] A few of the book productions with which Hultén was closely associated are undoubtedly based on *book art* and *art in book form*. Lutz Jahre, for instance, writes that Hultén said that a good, fine book had a non-commercial side, a generous side that is *Art Extra*.[6] Hultén himself wrote that he read a great deal about different artistic disciplines, both to relax and for inspiration, stating that, "A catalogue is a book, and a book is an object, an object that has character and individuality in its own right."[7]

This essay is based on the books that Pontus Hultén donated to Moderna Museet in 2005. The purpose is to identify a few of the influences and themes that have been significant to Hultén's practice as a museum director, catalogue producer and book collector. The following subjects will be highlighted: art historian Alfred

H. Barr, the first director of the Museum of Modern Art (MoMA) between 1929 and 1943; the Dada and Surrealist interest in combining image and language in various publications, including books, periodicals and pamphlets; the obvious references to Marcel Duchamp's practice and his collaboration with Mary Reynolds; the Fluxus movement and Concrete Poetry in the 1960s.

The library

Pontus Hultén donated his library, comprising some 137 shelf metres, or some 7,000 books, to Moderna Museet, to make it accessible to the public in a suitable way and to be used for education and research.[8] The donation was accompanied by an inventory list of titles, under the following headings: Artist Biographies, General/Survey Exhibition Catalogues, Artists' Books, Photography, Museum Handbooks, Design, Typography, Music, Museum as Subject, Machine as Art, Exposition Catalogues, Architecture, Cinema, Art Reference, Art General: Geographic, Miscellanous, and Art History: Chronological, Criticism.[9] This list gives a good idea of Pontus Hultén's overall fields of interest as a museum director, as we know them today. In his library, more established art history vied for space with new developments in visual and book arts taking place during his lifetime.[10]

Several volumes in the book collection are exhibition catalogues from museums where Hultén had worked, or gifts from institutions and individuals he knew or had collaborated with. As for the artists represented, three general groups could be distinguished. The first consists of older practices that were canonised in the 20th century and were considered to have developed new movements in art, such as Giuseppe Arcimboldo, Piero della Francesca, Francisco de Goya and Johannes Vermeer.[11] The latter was also the subject for Hultén's licentiate degree paper, *Vermeer och Spinoza* in 1951.[12] The second category consists of artists with whom Hultén had a more personal relationship or close friendship, and whom he helped establish in one way or another, including Sam Francis, Claes Oldenburg, Niki de Saint Phalle, Robert Rauschenberg, Jean Tinguely and Andy Warhol.[13] The third group is artists who were either prominent at the time the books were published, or who have become more or less famous later on, including Jean-Paul Riopelle, the pioneer of Spontaneism in the 1950s, and the artist duo Gilbert & George.[14]

Above: Cover of *Clic*, 688 photographs by Leonardo Bezzola, Solothurn: Edition mb&t, 1978. Below: Dedication from Bernhard Luginbühl and Jean Tinguely to Pontus Hultén in *Clic*, 1978

In addition, there are a few books that can be classified as both literature and art objects. The inventory lists some 340 book covers and first pages under the Artists' Books heading, copied and arranged in alphabetical order by surname.[15] Some of the books in this category could be regarded both as being about or by an artist, and artists' books, which Leif Eriksson, the Swedish doyen in this field, translated as *konst i bokform* ("art in the form of a book" in Swedish).[16] Several of the artists' books in Pontus Hultén's donation are linked to artists who pioneered conceptual art and art in a broader sense. The medium itself and its usually smaller format offered artists new potential to interact more directly with viewers. In their various practices, the artists created unique objects, one-offs or editions, working both with traditional methods and with new materials and printing techniques. Eriksson, for instance, relates the book's design and contents, but not necessarily its lexicality, to a visual, artistic style that emcompasses both a conceptual and idea-based practice. Hultén was strongly influenced by Duchamp's views on the creative act as taking place in the context of the spectator.[17] In his own practice, Hultén participated in producing objects that position themselves in the field between the concepts of artists' books and book art which is a broader term for book design.[18]

Alfred H. Barr and the Museum of Modern Art

A few of the seminal influences behind Pontus Hultén's directorship came from across the Atlantic, from the United States. Alfred H. Barr has most probably impacted on Hultén's notions of what a modern art museum should be.[19] Barr's ideas served as a matrix for how many modern museums were organised in the post-war era, along with his views on the exhibition as a medium, as exemplified by his exhibitions *Cubism and Abstract Art* (1936), and *Fantastic Art, Dada, Surrealism* (1936–37).[20] The artists Barr presented in the catalogues have subsequently been featured regularly by museum directors and curators all over the world, in both monographic and thematic shows. Despite being somewhat critical of MoMA in the catalogue for the exhibition *Stedelijk Meets Moderna Museet* (1962), Barr's exhibition catalogues indicated an art historic pathway that Hultén subsequently kept to throughout his career.[21]

Barr's exhibition *Machine Art* in 1934 clearly sparked Hultén's penchant for art and technology. This was expressed, for instance in *Movement in Art* (1961) at the Stedelijk Museum and Moderna Museet, *The Machine as Seen at the End of the Mechanical Age* (1968) at MoMA, and *New York Collection for Stockholm* (1973), where a special committee within *Experiments in Art and Technology* (E.A.T.), decided to put together a portfolio of prints to finance the Moderna Museet project.[22] The first two exhibitions were accompanied by a catalogue each. Both were unique in their own way – one with its tall, oblong format, the other with its metal-plated covers with relief print.

Pontus Hultén's library includes two copies of Barr's catalogue *Fantastic Art, Dada, Surrealism*. One is a first edition from 1936. Its green covers are rather faded and worn.[23] The other, a third edition from 1968 with brown-beige covers, is practically in mint condition. In the foreword to the first edition, Barr states that Surrealism is much more than an art movement. It is a serious matter, a philosophy, a way of life, embraced by several of the most brilliant painters and poets of the time.[24] When Hultén was the editor of *The Surrealists Look At Art* (1990), published by Sam Francis' company Lapis Press, with essays by such Surrealist trailblazers as Paul Éluard, Louis Aragon, Philippe Soupault, André Breton and Tristan Tzara, he ended his preface with the words: "Where do we find such passion, such poetic beauty of language? The reasoning might seem biased and out of fashion, and it sometimes is, but it is never journalistic, constipated, shallow or dull."[25] It is reasonable to assume that the first edition of Barr's catalogue served as an encyclopaedia for Hultén as a young art historian who was keen to keep up with the latest in art, and also a guide that he referred to regularly throughout his later career. When Hultén began studying art history in 1945, the catalogue and exhibition were only ten years old. The concept of linking historic and contemporary material, as Hultén did in the first exhibition he curated himself, *Movement in Art*, had been formulated already in the preface to the Surrealist and Dada catalogue. Barr wrote that even the incidental spectator will notice similarities between the older material presented and certain works in Dada and Surrealism.

The catalogue included works by Jean Arp. One of these works is created by an underlying page being visible through an opening in the covering sheet.[26] In this way, two works become three, or, alternatively, one. This design principle is repeated in the cover for Emmett Williams' *Material 3. Konkretionen* (1958), edited by Daniel Spoerri, who was involved in *Movement in Art*. Spoerri was also the

Cover for Bruno Munari, *Good Design*, Milan:
All'Insegna del Pesce d'Oro (Vanni Scheiwiller), 1963

founder of Edition MAT in 1959, whose mission was to produce series of objects as affordably as possible, so-called multiples. The same solution, with a hole punched in the page so that the viewer can see the next page, recurs in the catalogue cover for the exhibition *New York Collection for Stockholm* in 1973. Three years earlier, the curator and artist Ragnar von Holten and the artist José Pierre, the unofficial historiographer of Surrealism, had used this device when designing the catalogue for the *Surrealism* exhibition in 1970, produced by Riksutställningar – the Swedish Exhibition Agency – and shown at Moderna Museet. A rectangle is cut out of the right-hand corner of the front cover. The page behind it bears the word *sur-rea-lism.*[27]

Dada, Surrealism and Marcel Duchamp

Dada and Surrealist play with images, words, sounds, typography and all matter of paraphernalia feature consistently also in the catalogues Pontus Hultén produced. The Dadaists and Surrealists often made a virtue of necessity, using the materials available to them, since they were active during and between the two world wars. This eventually became a design ideology, demonstrating the importance of adapting aesthetic styles to technical and material resources. The Dada exhibition at Moderna Museet in 1966 was organised by the Friends of Moderna Museet. Newsletter number 19 from the Friends contains a documentation of the birthday party, a poetry reading on the evening of 3 February, held in memory of the founding of Cabaret Voltaire in 1916, the club in Zürich where Dadaism began. Pontus Hultén concluded his introduction in the newsletter:

> How liberating it is to look at a Dada work of art or read Dada texts, what purity and intelligence is radiated by most of what was written and made in the Dada circles! To experience the Dada clarity inspires an intellectual rush of joy. And nothing could be more inspiring.[28]

There is a handful of books about Dada in Pontus Hultén's library. In *The Dada Painters and Poets. An Anthology* (1951), someone has written "Hultén's". Two-hundred and sixty-six pages later, the following passage has been circled and marked with an asterisk in the margin:

> The meeting of *391* and Dada was celebrated in new issues of *391* and of *The Dada Review*. *391* appeared on bright pink paper. Arp, Tzara, Picabia and myself [Hans Richter] contributed to the two magazines, not only with individual work but by the execution in common of an illustration for Dada Nos. 3 and 4. Every detail of this illustration is still fresh in my mind. The medium was an old alarm clock which we bought for a few cents and took apart. The detached pieces were bathed in ink and then imprinted on random paper. All of us watched over the execution of this automatic masterpiece.[29]

Regardless of who highlighted the above passage, it points at ways of collaborating where coincidence and collective artistic work are the guiding factors for producing a book, a magazine or work of art. It also distinctly suggests an expanded use of different kinds of paper: coloured, irregularly cut, folded and punched in various ways, as in the catalogue for *American Pop Art. 106 Forms of Love and Despair* (1964). Paper, for instance, is the fundamental principle of the artists' books by Bruno Munari and Richard Long, which Pontus Hultén donated to the collection.[30] Hultén mentions Munari in *Kasark* (1955), referring to his *proiezoni dirette*, breathtakingly simple moving images without being film, which Hultén had noted at MoMA.[31]

Coloured prints of various kinds, along with a mixture of typefaces were standard features in several of the catalogues Hultén participated in producing in the 1960s. The initials and type area are sometimes redolent of the days when each page was cut in wood and printed like a stamp, before Johannes Gutenberg introduced his revolutionary invention of reusable types. For the 500th anniversary of Gutenberg's invention, Hans Nordenström embarked on a four-minute film titled *Det tryckta ordet, 500 år med Gutenberg* (The Printed Word, 500 years with Gutenberg, 1949), with Hultén assisting him.[32] Hultén's interest in printing and books was manifested early in his career. His association with Bok Konsum (bookshop and gallery space in Stockholm during the 1960s), *Galleri Samlaren*, *Kasark* (magazine) and *Blandaren* (a magazine produced by students at KTH, the Royal Institute of Technology, Stockholm), which were all considered more radical platforms on the alternative art scene, have rendered him a place in the avant-garde in Swedish contemporary art historiography.[33] From the perspective of youthful opposition to the bourgeoisie, Hultén adheres to a given tradition

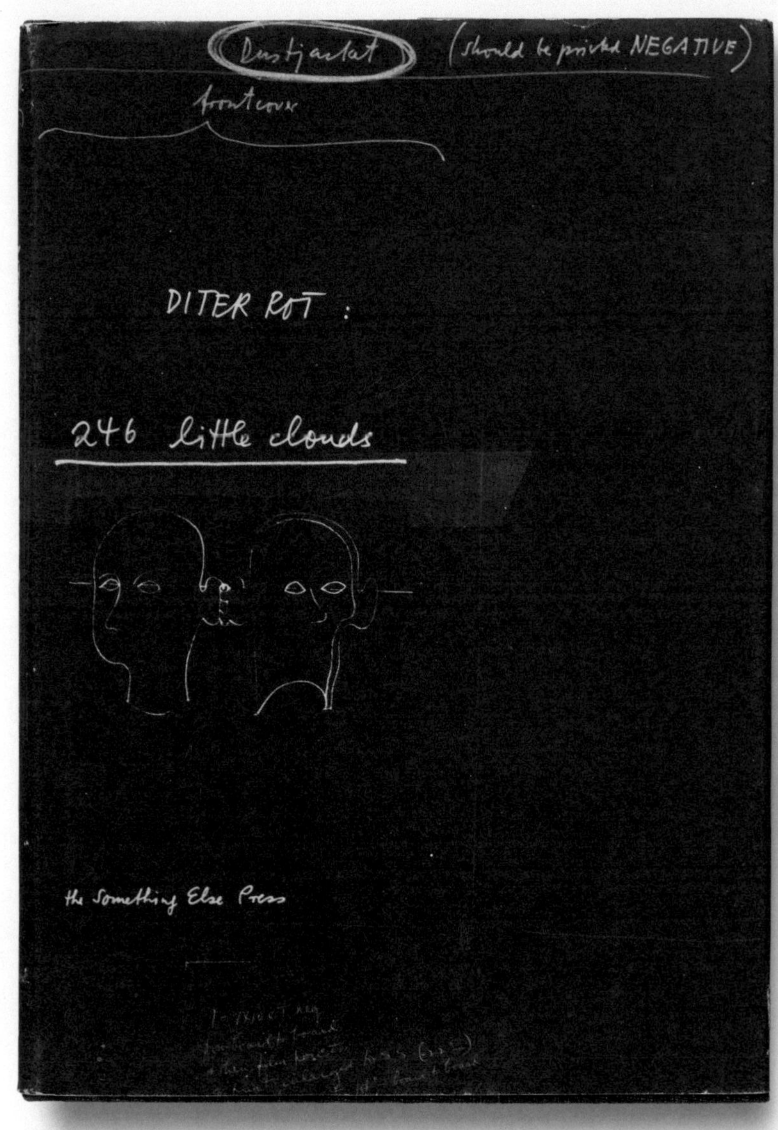

Cover of Diter Rot, *246 Little Clouds*, New York: Something Else Press, 1965

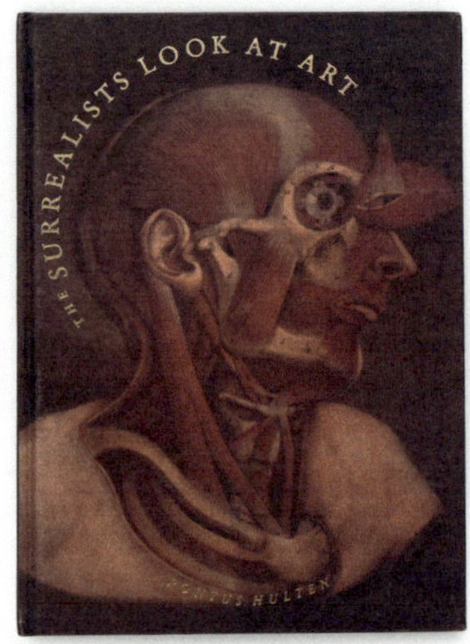

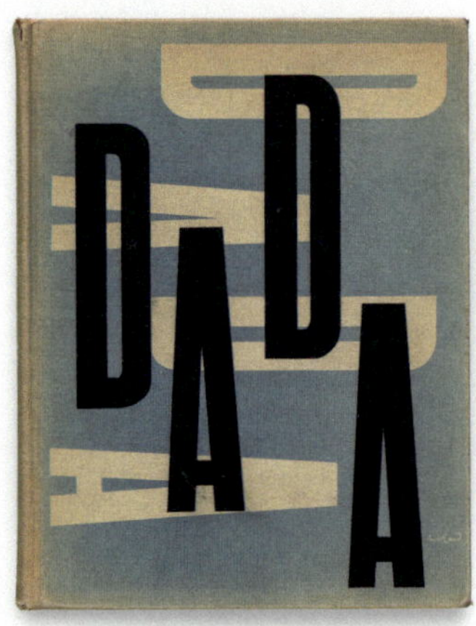

Above: Edward Hugh and Marcel Duchamp, *Surrealism and Its Affinities. Mary Reynolds Collection*, Chicago: Art Institute Chicago, 1956. *The Surrealists Look at Art*, ed. Pontus Hultén, Culver City: Lapis Press, 1990. Below: Karl-Heinz Hering, *DADA. Dokumente eine Bewegung*, Düsseldorf: Kunstverein für die Rheinlande und Westfalen, 1958. *The Dada Painters and Poets. An Anthology*, ed. Robert Motherwell, New York: Wittenborn, Schultz Inc., 1951

of pamphlets and manifestos with roots in the 19th century.[34] Willem Sandberg, director of the Stedelijk Museum in Amsterdam between 1945 and 1963, was also a graphic designer. In Vienna, he had studied the philosopher and sociologist Otto Neurath's picture language Isotype. This is a theme that runs through Sandberg's entire publication *NU*.[35] Hultén's more explicit choice of Sandberg as his mentor, rather than Barr, is more in line with the existing exchange of experiences between the Nationalmuseum in Sweden and the Rijksmuseum in the Netherlands.[36] Hultén took after Sandberg's practice and took part in the process of producing the museum's publications, in close collaboration with the editor Georg Svensson and the printer Gösta Svensson (they were not related), the designer John Melin, and the advertising executive Anders Österlin, among others.

Pontus Hultén's interest in book design can also be related to the bookbinder Mary Reynolds' works, which were presented in an exhibition catalogue in 1956, six years after her death.[37] Marcel Duchamp, who lived with Reynolds for many years, begins his preface by describing how she had witnessed the Dada manifestations and the birth of Surrealism in 1924. Duchamp ends his tribute to Reynolds by writing that her book bindings were original and unlike classical techniques. Mary Reynolds' collaboration with Marcel Duchamp between 1924 and 1935 on Alfred Jarry's drama *Ubu Roi* from 1896 is a typical example of approaching a book as an object. Pontus Hultén's various catalogue productions, such as the above-mentioned metal-covered catalogue for *The Machine as Seen at the End of the Mechanical Age* (1968), is a logical part of a tradition of more experimental book design, and artistic collaboration.[38]

Publishing *Boulevardkartongen Tvångsblandaren* (1955–56), also known as *Kartongblandaren*, as a cardboard box with loose pages rather than as a stapled magazine was also a sign of the times. In the 1950s, Hans Nordenström was the editor and primary driving force of *Blandaren*. In his preface to Nordenström's book *Brul: Svart-Vit Magi* (2002), Hultén writes that Marcel Duchamp's *La Boîte-en-valise* (1935–41) provided the inspiration for *Boulevardkartongen*, which was "an expression of enormous admiration for Duchamp".[39] It is well-known that Duchamp was especially significant in Hultén's version of art history. The terse, witty correspondence between the two gentlemen bears witness of this, as do the many exhibitions in which Hultén presented Duchamp, and the 86 books relating directly to Duchamp in Hultén's library.[40] These include a first edition of Wassily Kandinsky's *Über das Geistige in der Kunst* (Concerning the Spiritual in Art, 1911), in which a young Duchamp has attempted to translate various passages from German into French. In his preface to the Nordenström book, Hultén emphasises the similarities with the famous Dada method 30 years previously; unlike Dada, however, the Blandaren team simply wanted to get the issue done on time, according to Hultén. *Kartongblandaren* also has references to an era when royalty and other wealthy collectors kept loose prints, drawings, drafts and sketches in albums, cassettes and boxes made of various materials, similar to the E.A.T. portfolio discussed above.

In the case of *Tvångsblandaren*, there are several versions regarding who inspired whom and what. The journalist and artist Leif Nylén writes:

> George Maciunas later tried to recruit Hans Nordenström to Fluxus. The reason may have been *Boulevardkartongen Tvångsblandaren*, the 1955 issue of the student magazine Blandaren and something of a precursor to the Fluxus boxes. Nordenström, aka "Brul", was a legendary contributor to *Blandaren* – as its editor, he commissioned work from friends who were artists, writers and art historians, especially Per Olof Ultvedt and Pontus Hultén.[41]

The ethnologist and Fluxus artist Bengt af Klintberg claims:

> It is most likely that it was Duchamp who gave [George] Maciunas the idea for the Fluxboxes that were mass-produced a few years later in his New York loft, but he may also have been inspired by *Tvångsblandaren*. If so, *Tvångsblandaren* is worth a footnote in art history for pioneering a phenomenon that now goes by the name of multiple.[42]

With regard to *Tvångsblandaren,* there are also references to a new edition of André Breton's *Surrealist Manifesto* (1924). In the version published in 1955, a magnifying glass is included in a punched recess in the pages.[43] The picture of Duchamp's *Why Not Sneeze, Rrose Sélavy?* (1921) is accompanied by the text "PARENTS! racontez vos rêves à vos enfants, 45, rue de Grenelle. Paris-7e" in white against a black square. It is placed diagonally across the page, corresponding to the reproduction in black and white of Duchamp's work. The interest in Duchamp was also promoted at this time by a younger

Cover of *The Xerox Book*, New York: Seth Siegelaub, 1968

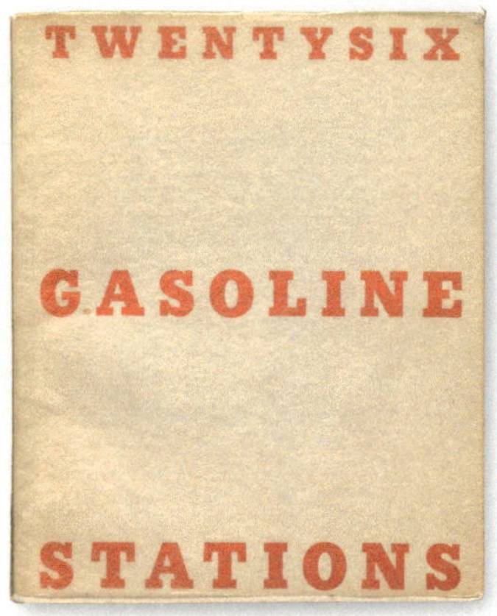

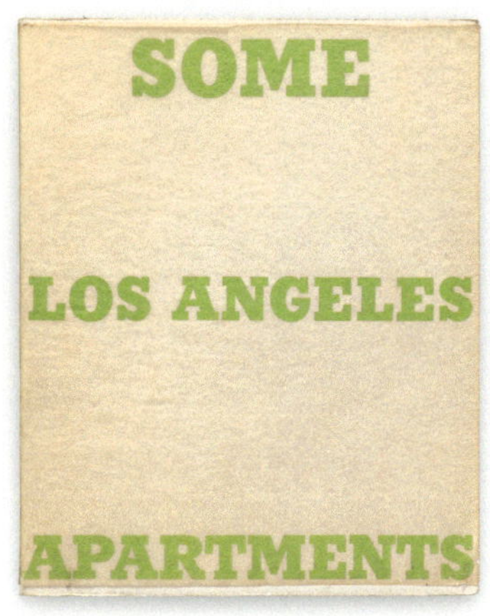

Above: Edward Ruscha, *Twentysix Gasoline Stations*, Los Angeles, 1963. Edward Ruscha, *Some Los Angeles Apartments,* Los Angeles, 1963. Below: Lawrence Weiner, *Statements*, New York: The Louis Kellner Foundation, 1968. Emmett Williams, *Sweethearts*, New York: Something Else Press, 1967

generation of artists, including John Cage, Merce Cunningham, Jasper Johns and Robert Rauschenberg, who all looked up to Marcel Duchamp as the origin of modern art. [44] That Duchamp became fashionable in the 1950s and onwards is a typical and traditional case of circular reasoning, where masters are said to generate masters, and followers themselves name their predecessors.

Fluxus and Concrete Poetry

In 1966, Dick Higgins, founder of the Something Else Press (1963–74), reissued a facsimile of Richard Huelsenbeck's *Dada Almanach*, first published in 1920. On the brown front cover, Higgins had written in yellow, "Dada is like the weather. Everybody talks about it, but nobody does anything about it."[45] Higgins wanted to change that. He wanted to demonstrate that the Dada approach *is always* contemporary. Otherwise, he said, it would be impossible to correctly evaluate most tendencies in philosophy and art at the time. Something Else Press also published intermedia works by a few Fluxus artists. Even before the term *conceptualism* was coined, many small publishers were presenting art in the form of publications, pamphlets and books, with design as a conceptual element in its own right. Some Fluxus pieces are represented in Hultén's library, including the above-mentioned *Material 3. Konkretionen* (1958). Another work is *246 Little Clouds* (1965) by Dieter Roth (also Diter Rot), with a foreword by Emmett Williams.[46] Roth, in turn, was the artist who designed the poster for *Movement in Art*. Its characteristic look, with punched holes, is repeated in Roth's *Bok 3b* (1961), which consists of cropped images from comics with holes punched in them.[47] These holes also refer, in some way, to the nine cannonball holes in Marcel Duchamp's work *La Mariée mis à nu par ses célibataires, même* (*Le Grand Verre*) from 1915–23.

Opinions differ on whether Fluxus existed in Sweden. Leif Nylén, for instance, considers Fluxus as artistic action to include more expressions than Bengt af Klintberg does. Bengt af Klintberg claims that Fluxus never gained a proper foothold in Sweden, as Pontus Hultén and Moderna Museet were more focused on happenings.[48] Nylén writes that: "Swedish 1960s modernism was more attracted by technology and mass culture than by the poetic, Zen-influenced minimalism of Fluxus."[49] The Fluxus artists and conceptualists saw books as a democratic art form that could be shared to the masses.

Books could be used to spread their ideas and circumvent the art gallerists.

Galleries were both an obstacle to what the artists and art historians (later defined as curators) perceived as a free market, and a necessary condition for the platforms they used to gain more exposure on the art scene in general.[50] The gallerists eventually came to embrace the concept of artists' books as publishers. One example of this is the collaboration between artist Ed Ruscha and the gallerist Leo Castelli. Ruscha produced his first artist's book, *Twentysix Gasoline Stations*, on his own in 1962. The same year, Ruscha was featured in a solo exhibition at the Stedelijk Museum in Amsterdam. Thirty-five years later, Castelli published Ruscha's *Cityscapes O Books* (1997). Annie Cohen-Solal quotes Ruscha in her biography on Leo Castelli (2010), in which Ruscha relates that he met Castelli in Los Angeles in 1961, but that Castelli didn't start showing his works until ten years later.[51]

Pontus Hultén's library also includes Ed Ruscha's *Various Small Fires and Milk* (1964), *Some Los Angeles Apartments* (1965), *Records* (1971) and *Colored People* (1972). Two other books that have also achieved cult status today are Lawrence Weiner's *Statements* and *The Xerox Book*, with works by Carl Andre, Robert Barry, Douglas Huebler, Joseph Kosuth, Sol Lewitt, Robert Morris and Lawrence Weiner, both from 1968.[52] The above works are all examples of artists' books that are found in libraries and museum collections worldwide. They demonstrate that the sibling disciplines of art and literature can treat these objects as literature, artefact or art, but that the artistic practice or the work as a whole is rarely influenced by the place where the book/artwork is stored, collected or shown.

The library includes a copy of Öyvind Fahlström's revised manifesto for Concrete Poetry, first published in 1954, in the journal *Odyssé*, no. 2–3.[53] Concrete Poetry had a privileged position at Moderna Museet, and, albeit on a smaller scale, on Hultén's bookshelves. The exhibition *Svisch – En manifestation* took place at Moderna Museet from 26 September to 18 October, 1964. In conjunction with the exhibition, the authors were featured in evenings with image-sound-poetry on 7 and 14 October and 4 November.[54] A clear example of concrete art in book form is the accordion book *Ett ord på vägen* (1964), published by Åke Hodell's publishing house Kerberos (1963–72) in conjunction with the Soviet premier Nikita Khrushchev's visit to Sweden that year.[55] Åke Hodell, Leif Nylén, Carl Fredrik Reuterswärd, Bengt

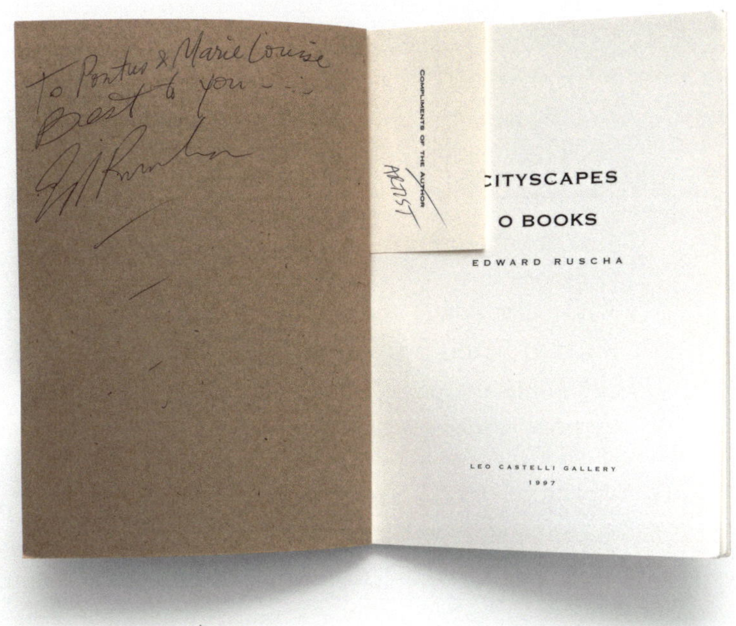

Above: Cover of Edward Ruscha, *Cityscapes O Books*, New York: Leo Castelli Gallery, 1997. Below: Dedication from Edward Ruscha to Pontus Hultén and Marie-Louise von Plessen

Emil Johnson, Mats G. Bengtsson, Lars-Gunnar Bodin, Per Olof Ultvedt, Öyvind Fahlström and Elis Eriksson contributed Concrete Poetry and texts for the work. The library also includes a few books by Torsten Ekbom, Jarl Hammarberg, Åke Hodell and Carl Fredrik Reuterswärd. The publishing company Albert Bonniers Förlag published Concrete Poetry by Hammarberg and Reuterswärd, albeit in more traditionally bound volumes.

Innovation or tradition is largely defined by the context. One long continuous *svisch* stretches across the front cover of *Ett ord på vägen*, leading the viewer on to the next page, where Torsten Ekbom quotes John Cage on beauty, as a starting point for a discussion proposing that everyone can learn to see. The same attitude to understanding art is also substantiated by Bror Ejve, the head of Konstfrämjandet, the Swedish organization for promoting art. He begins his preface for one of Konstfrämjandet's catalogues with the words "everybody is taught how to read", and goes on to propose that everyone should also have the opportunity to learn to see.[56] The visual and verbal expressions of Dada and Concrete Poetry respectively have obvious points in common. However, the similarities between the modernist focus on artistic norm-breaking and the contemporary promotion of art rooted in older learning traditions have not been discussed as thoroughly. For instance, Per Olov Ultvedt had been involved in Konstfrämjandet's art education activities before he began working with Pontus Hultén, a fact that is rarely mentioned in relation to the work they undertook together.[57]

Two sides of the same coin

Throughout most of the 20th century, art history dealt mainly with the time before the beginning of the previous century. It is understandable, therefore, that Pontus Hultén's peers perceived several of his book and exhibition productions as entirely innovative and practically unrelated to what else was going on in the West. Today, we can identify predecessors, references, fashions and trends, and also discuss these on the basis of new research on networks consisting of people, exhibitions and publications. Hultén himself belonged to several predominantly male networks, which reflected one another more or less directly. He migrated continuously between different positions within these networks, which meant that he could both adhere closely to his predecessors and follow his contemporary colleagues. Sometimes, he would realise ideas that were more his own, and sometimes, he borrowed directly off from others.

The books in Hultén's library are there for reasons we can only speculate about, but they prove that he often had access to the knowledge they contained (even if he did not know what was written in them and/or what had been written about them or used it). They also show that he was not strictly a book collector, but that he collected books and art in the form of books. Hultén and his library are firmly rooted in what was art history then and what has come to be art history today. Hultén the traditional art historian, visible in the art historic references that the library presents, and Hultén the curator, whom art historians today refer to in various texts about the curatorial profession as it is or will become, are two sides of the same coin. In addition to marking social status and manifesting a cultural position, the library is an excellent source for further research into the form and content of books as art and books about art in the second half of the 20th century.

1. Carl Nordenfalk, the director who promoted Hultén to the directorship of Moderna Museet, also had a private library. He had some 200 books in his specialist field, mediaeval manuscripts; they are now in the Art Library. E-mail to the author from Maria Sylvén, Head of the Art Library, 2 August, 2018. See also Carl Nordenfalk, *Mest om konst. Memoarer efter författarens efterlämnade manuskript,* eds. Katarina Nordenfalk and Per Bjurström, Vitterhetsakademiens serie Svenska lärde, Stockholm: Natur & Kultur, 1996.

2. Stuart Burch, *Introducing Mr Moderna Museet: Pontus Hultén and Sweden's Museum of Modern Art*, 2008, http://www.stuartburch.com/uploads/8/1/9/1/8191744/2012_-_introducing_mr_moderna_museet.pdf (23 August, 2022).

3. Lutz Jahre, "Ein Gespräch mit Pontus Hultén", *Das Gedruckte Museum von Pontus Hultén. Kunstastellungen und ihre Bücher*, Ostfildern-Ruit: Cantz Verlag, 1996, pp. 11–28 Martin Sundberg, "Between Experiment and Everyday Life. The Exhibition Catalogues of Moderna Museet", *The History Book. On Moderna Museet 1958–2008*, eds. Anna Tellgren and Martin Sundberg, Stockholm: Moderna Museet and Göttingen: Steidl, 2008, pp. 297–328.

4. Lutz Jahre, "Über Austellungskataloge", *Das Gedruckte Museum von Pontus Hultén*, 1996, pp. 173–177.

5. K. G. Pontus Hultén, *Jean Tinguely. Méta*, eds. Berit Tärnlund and Katja Waldén, Stockholm: Moderna Museet, 1972. The book is designed with a handle on the spine, so it can be carried like a briefcase. It has a small clasp with a key, like a diary used for writing secret thoughts in. The book also contains a vinyl record and a bound drawing made with a *Méta-matic*. Three years after it was published in Swedish, editions of 250 were printed in London by Thames and Hudson (Series A) and in New York by the New York Graphic Society (Series B). This relates, for instance, to the different series that were made of Duchamp's *La Boîte-en-valise*.

6. Lutz Jahre, "Ein Gespräch mit Pontus Hultén", *Das Gedruckte Museum von Pontus Hultén*, 1996, p. 27.

7. Pontus Hultén, "Über Austellungskataloge", *Das Gedruckte Museum von Pontus Hultén,* 1996, p. 177. Original text: "Ein Katalog ist ein Buch, und ein Buch is ein Gegenstand, ein Gegenstand mit seinem eigenen Recht auf Charakter und Individualität."

8. Donation letter dated 3 August, 2005, Reg. no. 2005-23-105. MMA MA F2d:35. Anna Tellgren, "Pontus Hultén and Moderna Museet. Research and learning based on an art collection, an archive and a library", *Pontus Hultén and Moderna Museet. The Formative Years*, ed. Anna Tellgren and Anna Lundström, Stockholm: Moderna Museet and London: Koenig Books, 2017, p. 26. To digitise the library and make it searchable, the archive assistant Linda Andersson worked part-time for two years (2016–2017) on reviewing and cataloguing most of the library. She managed to catalogue 6,821 volumes according to title, artist, author, subject, publisher, publishing date, size and ISBN, and organised the books roughly into three categories: artist, country and general art history. The work to cataloguing the library has continued during 2020–2021, primarily on books from France, Sweden, Germany and

the US. Some volumes with folders and small printed matter remain to be catalogued.

9. Boksamlingen, Book register. MMA PHA 5.3. The archive material does not state who created these categories. Ann Goldstein states that she organised Pontus Hultén's library in 1983–1984, when Hultén was director of MOCA. See Ann Goldstein, "Director of Intelligence: Daniel Birnbaum, Ann Goldstein and Daniel Buren on Pontus Hultén", *Artforum*, vol. 45, no. 6, 2007, pp. 62–65.

10. How, where and when Pontus Hultén acquired all his books has not been ascertained at this time. It is possible to make some (more or less certain) assumptions based on publishing date, type of volume, subject and dedications. Some of the books from Hultén's library mentioned in this essay, for instance, are unopened. Even so, we can assume that Hultén has been able to read the books mentioned, if not his own copies, then at other institutions or on the market.

11. Giuseppe Arcimboldo (2 volumes), Piero della Francesca (3 volumes), Francisco de Goya (5 volumes), Johannes Vermeer (11 volumes). The number of volumes refers to the books about each respective artist included in the donation, not to how many Hultén acquired or was given during his lifetime. Nevertheless, it gives an idea of the reference material Hultén would have had at his disposal.

12. Egna verk, Text, Färdigt manuskript, *Vermeer och Spinoza*, 1951. MMA PHA 2.10–12. The manuscript was later published in French translated by Lydie Rousseau: Pontus Hultén, *Vermeer et Spinoza*, Paris: Échoppe, 2002.

13. Sam Francis (52 volumes), Claes Oldenburg (36 volumes), Niki de Saint Phalle (41 volumes), Robert Rauschenberg (16 volumes), Jean Tinguely (17 volumes), Andy Warhol (32 volumes). There is no absolute correlation between the number of volumes and Hultén's personal or professional involvement with the artist. For instance, Hultén featured works by Rauschenberg in five major exhibitions: *Movement in Art* (1961), *Four Americans* (1962), *Inner and Outer Space* (1965), *New York Collection for Stockholm* (1973), and *Territorium Artis* (1992). He also showed George Brecht, Alexander Calder, Marcel Duchamp, Viking Eggeling, Alberto Giacometti, Kazimir Malevich, Francis Picabia, Man Ray, Niki de Saint Phalle and Jean Tinguely in *Movement in Art* and *Territorium Artis*.

14. Jean-Paul Riopelle (5 volumes), Gilbert & George (2 volumes).

15. Boksamlingen, Book Register, Artists' Books A–Z. MMA PHA 5.3. A consecutive number is hand-written on each photocopy. The numerical series deviates here and there, as more books have been added. When or how this happened cannot be deduced from the numerical order or any other documentation on Hultén's library that I have found so far in his archives. It is possible that some of the books listed as artists' books were not included in the donation. In connection with the donation in 2005, an inventory was made of all the art objects, including 53 books/objects that were classified and registered as artists' books in the Moderna Museet collection. No explanation was noted as to why some of the books in the

donation have inventory numbers and others remained in the library, nor why some of the artists' books in the inventory were not included in the list of artists' books. Therefore, some books/objects may belong in both the library and in Moderna Museet's collection of art. For the time being, we have chosen not to transfer objects/books between the library and object collection, since it is possible to search by either author/artist or title in both the archive and art databases.

16. Leif Eriksson, *Konst i bokform*, Stockholm: Föreningen Svenska Tecknare, 1998. For further discussions on the concept of artists' books and their history, see: *Artists' Books: A Critical Anthology and Sourcebook*, ed. Joan Lyons, New York: Visual Studies Workshop Press, 1985; Johanna Drucker, *The Century of Artists' Books*, New York: Granary Books, 1994/2004; Stefan Klima, *Artists' Books: A Critical Survey of the Literature*, New York: Granary Books, 1998; Sune Nordgren, "Konstnärsböcker, Artists' Books", *Kalejdoskop*, no. 1–2, 1980; Germano Celant, *Book as Artwork 1960/1970*, London: Nigel Greenwood Inc. Ltd., 1972. See also Thomas Millroth, *Artists' Books from a Swedish Point of View with Special Attention Paid to the Contributions of Denmark and GDR*, Lund: Ellerströms and Stockholm: Tragus, 2021.

17. Marcel Duchamp, "The Creative Act", *Marcel Duchamp. Salt Seller*, eds. Michel Sanouillet and Elmer Peterson, New York: Oxford University Press, 1973, or listen to Marcel Duchamp reading *The Creative Act*: http://www.openculture.com/2015/10/hear-marcel-duchamp-read-the-creative-act.html (23 August, 2022).

18. Today, researchers and artists pay equal attention to the actual publishing process and the object that it produces when addressing what is art. See, for instance: *Publishing as Artistic Practice*, ed. Annette Gilbert, London: Sternberg Press Ltd, 2016.

19. Bernadette Dufrêne, "La muséologie selon Pontus Hultén", *Les Cahiers du Musée national d'art moderne*, Paris: Éditions du Centre Pompidou, no. 141, autumn 2017, p. 61.

20. *Cubism and Abstract Art* (2 March–19 April, 1936) and *Fantastic Art, Dada, Surrealism* (9 December, 1936–17 January, 1937). Sybil Gordon Kantor, *Alfred H. Barr Jr. Intellectual Origins of the Museum of Modern Art*, Cambridge, Massachusetts, and London: MIT Press, 2002.

21. Hultén writes that Barr was at MoMA before Willem Sandberg came to the Stedelijk, but that MoMA "maybe never managed to break through that wall of money, nobility and snobbery which they have to thank for their existence", K.G. Hultén, "Sandberg och Stedelijk Museum", *Stedelijk Museum, Amsterdam besöker Moderna Museet, Stockholm*, ed. Pontus Hultén, Moderna Museet exhibition catalogue no. 19, Stockholm: Moderna Museet, 1962, p. 5.

22. Annika Gunnarsson, "Sidetrack – Robert Rauschenberg", *Konsthistorisk tidskrift/Journal of Art History*, vol. 76, häfte 1–2, 2007, pp. 67–69.

23. The catalogue is available at: https://www.moma.org/calendar/exhibitions/2823 (23 August, 2022).

24. Alfred H. Barr, *Fantastic Art, Dada, Surrealism* (exh. cat.), ed. Alfred H. Barr, New York: The Museum of Modern Art, 1936, unpaginated preface.

25. Pontus Hultén, *The Surrealists Look at Art*, ed. Pontus Hultén, Culver City: Lapis Press, 1990, unpaginated preface.

26. *Fantastic Art, Dada, Surrealism*, 1936, pp. 276–277.

27. There are further parallels between this particular catalogue and Pontus Hultén's own catalogue production. The cover for Riksutställningar's Surrealism catalogue is adorned with the portrait of *The Librarian* (1566) by Giuseppe Arcimboldo. Hultén's catalogue for the exhibition *The Arcimboldo Effect: Transformations of the Face from the 16th to the 20th Century* (1987) has on the cover Arcimboldo's *Vertumnus* (c. 1590–91), an allegorical portrait of Rudolf II, Holy Roman Emperor. This painting is in the collection of Skokloster Castle. Olle Granath mentions that he assisted Pontus Hultén in borrowing this work for the exhibition. See *Pontus Hultén på Moderna Museet. Vittnesseminarium, Södertörns högskola, 26 april 2017*, eds. Charlotte Bydler, Andreas Gedin and Johanna Ringarp, Samtidshistoriska frågor 38, Huddinge: Södertörn University, 2018, p. 25.

28. Karl Gunnar Hultén, "Introduktion", *Meddelande från Moderna Museet till Moderna Museets Vänner,* eds. Thomas Hall and Ingrid Svensson, no. 19, March 1966, p. 2.

29. Hans Richter, "Dada X Y Z", *The Dada Painters and Poets. An Anthology*, ed. Robert Motherwell, New York: Wittenborn, Schultz Inc., 1951, p. 266.

30. Bruno Munari, *The Quadrata-Prints*, 1953 (MOM/2005/548), *The Quadrata-Prints*, 1959 (MOM/2005/549), *The Quadrata-Prints*, 1959 (MOM/2005/550), and Richard Long, *Nile Papers of River Muds*, 1968–88 (MOM/2005/844).

31. Pontus Hultén, "Den ställföreträdande Friheten eller Om Rörelse i Konsten och Tinguelys metamekanik", *Kasark,* no. 2, October 1955, p. 24.

32. *Moderna Museet 1958–1983*, eds. Olle Granath and Monica Nieckels, Stockholm: Moderna Museet, 1983, p. 26. Johan Sundholm, professor of film studies at Stockholm University, confirms that the film has not been preserved. E-mail to the author from Andreas Bertman, Filmform, 21 August, 2018.

33. Andreas Gedin, *Pontus Hultén, Hon & Moderna*, Stockholm: Bokförlaget Langenskiöld, 2016, pp. 102–104. See also Patrik Andersson, "The Inner and the Outer Space. Rethinking movement in art", and Anna Lundström, "Movement in Art. The layers of an exhibition", *Pontus Hultén and Moderna Museet. The Formative Years*, 2017, p. 44, and pp. 71–74.

34. Janet Lyon, *Manifestos. Provocations of the Modern*, Ithaca and London: Cornell University Press, 1999.

35. Ank Leuwen Marcan, *Willem Sandberg. Portrait of an Artist*, Amsterdam: Valiz, 2013. Pontus Hultén's library included seven books relating to Willem Sandberg's typographic practice.

36. NM museum minutes, Statens Konstmuseeer and predecessors. Nationalmuseum's Central Administration (NMCK). NMA MA A 2:76–83.

37. Edward Hugh and Marcel Duchamp, *Surrealism and Its Affinities. Mary Reynolds Collection,* Chicago: Art Institute Chicago, 1956.

38. The Machine (MoMA). MMA PHA 4.2.52–55.

39. Pontus Hultén, "Blandaren" in Hans Nordenström, *Brul: Svart-Vit Magi*, Stockholm: Schultz Förlag, 2002, unpaginated preface.

40. Some of the correspondence is reproduced in *Meddelande från Moderna Museet till Moderna Museets Vänner*, eds. Thomas Hall and Ingrid Svensson, no. 19, March 1966.

41. Leif Nylén, *Den öppna konsten. Happenings, instrumental teater, konkret poesi och andra gränsöverskridningar i det svenska 60-talet*, Publication 107, Stockholm: Sveriges Allmänna Konstförening, 1998, pp. 45–46.

42. Bengt af Klintberg, *Svensk Fluxus = Swedish Fluxus*, Stockholm: Rönnells Antikvariat, 2006, p. 93.

43. André Breton, *Les Manifestes du surréalisme suivis de prolégomènes à un troisième manifeste du surréalisme ou non du surréalisme en ses œuvres vives et d'éphémérides surréalistes*, Paris: Le Sagittaire, 1955.

44. *Dancing around the Bride: Cage, Cunningham, Johns, Rauschenberg, and Duchamp* (exh. cat.), ed. Carlos Basualdo, New Haven: Yale University Press, 2013.

45. *Dada Almanach*, New York: Something Else Press,1966, facsimile of Richard Huelsenbeck, *Dada Almanach*, Berlin: Erich Reiss Verlag, 1920.

46. Dieter Roth, *246 Little Clouds*, New York: Something Else Press, 1965.

47. Dieter Roth, *Bok 3b*, 1961 (MOM/2005/864).

48. Bengt af Klintberg, *Svensk Fluxus*, 2006, p. 94.

49. Leif Nylén, *Den öppna konsten*, 1998, p. 37.

50. The market is often referred to as an obstacle preventing independent curators from working with art. See, for instance, *Pontus Hultén på Moderna Museet*, 2018, p. 101–103.

51. Annie Cohen-Solal, *Leo and His Circle. The Life of Leo Castelli*, New York: Alfred A. Knopf, 2010, p. 342.

52. Lawrence Weiner, *Statements*, New York: The Louis Kellner Foundation, 1968, and *The Xerox Book*, New York: Seth Siegelaub, 1968. Sara Mottalini, writes that *Statements*: "wonderfully fulfilled the artist's original intent for art to bypass the elitist model of the gallery, upend society's pre-conceived notions of what constitutes art, and both be available and accessible to the masses" in Sarah Mottalini, *Artists' Books: Where to Put the Apostrophe?,* January–April, 2015, Lally Reading Room at Schaffer Library, Union College, 2015, p. 2.

53. Öyvind Fahlström "Manifest", *Odyssé,* no. 2–3, spring 1954, unpaginated. Contributors were Öyvind Fahlström, Alfred Jarry, Gösta Kriland, Ilmar Laaban, Francis Picabia, Markis de Sade and Pär Wistrand. See Per Bäckström, "Öyvind Fahlströms konkreta poesi: Materialitet och performance", *Aiolos,* no. 42, 2011, pp. 75–82.

54. Leif Nylén, *Den öppna konsten,* 1998, p. 84.

55. *Svisch. Ett ord på vägen*, Stockholm: Kerberos, 1964.

56. Bror Ejve, "Förord", *Folkrörelsernas Konstfrämjande, utställning av*

originallitografier i färg, Stockholm, 1948, unpaginated. See Annika Gunnarsson, "Konstförståelse eller konstförströelse", *Konstfrämjandet 70 år*, ed. Niklas Östholm, Stockholm: Folkrörelsernas Konstfrämjande, 2017, p. 88.

57. Sandro Key Åberg, "Med konstfrämjandet för konsten", ed. Elisabeth Lidén, *Konst för alla? Konstfrämjandet 40 år*, Stockholm: Prins Eugens Waldemarsudde, 1987, and Annika Gunnarsson, "Konstförståelse eller konstförströelse", *Konstfrämjandet 70 år*, 2017, pp. 80 and 105.

A NEW ART SCHOOL IN PARIS

Daniel Buren, *Signe contre-signes: A. R. T.* (1972/1990) in the exhibition *Le Territoire de l'Art*, the Russian Museum, Leningrad, 1990

A New Art School in Paris. Institut des Hautes Études en Arts Plastiques

Anna Lundström

In 1982, when Jacques Chirac was the mayor of Paris, he gave Pontus Hultén the assignment of starting an art school in the city.[1] Institut des Hautes Études en Arts Plastiques (IHEAP) was long known by its working title, École de Paris, and the purpose was, at least as far as the city was concerned, to resurrect Paris as an artistic and cultural hub. The Institute opened on 4 October, 1988.[2] The studies that Hultén developed had an unconventional curriculum. Instead of studio-based work, instruction consisted exclusively of seminar-like discussions on themes that were explored for an entire year. These discussions were led by Hultén and its three permanent professors – the artist Daniel Buren, who took over as director in 1994–95, the art historian Serge Fauchereau, and the artist Sarkis – and invited guest lecturers consisting of artists, writers, philosophers, critics, solicitors and historians. These included Michael Asher, Pierre Bourdieu, Coosje Van Bruggen, Benjamin Buchloh, Dan Graham, Hans Haacke, Jean-François Lyotard, Jean-Hubert Martin, Claes Oldenburg, Renzo Piano, Yvonne Rainer, Niki de Saint Phalle, Harald Szeemann, and Jean Tinguely. The guest lecturers were invited to two-month residencies at the Institute.[3] The list is impressive, to say the least, although it should be noted that the four leaders were all men, and that the guests were predominantly male.

Pontus Hultén wanted the Institute to offer an environment underpinned by a few essential elements. The school should attract young artists who were at the beginning of their career (aged 20 to 30) from different parts of the world, for a one-year study period.[4] The educational activities were aimed to encourage interdisciplinary collaborations, exemplified by painting, sculpture, architecture, photography, music, drama and literature. There would also be room for reflection, debate and research.[5] The Institute was modelled on the forums of antiquity and renaissance academies, places where different forms of knowledge and experience were shared.[6] The ambition was to offer a place for reflective approaches. This is explained in one of the many programme declarations found in the Moderna Museet archives: "Based on the axiom that before being a technician, a skilled professional, the artist is someone who reflects on and feels concerned about the world and life; the studies offered by the institute seek to encourage doing without prejudice."[7] The core of the curriculum was exchange between students, professors and invited guest lecturers. The day-long discussions three times a week were complemented by a shared meal, which was emphasised repeatedly as being important.[8]

The schools referred to as models were L'Académie Matisse in France in the early 1900s, the Bauhaus in Germany in the 1920s and 1930s, and Black Mountain College in the United States in the 1950s.[9] References have also been made to the IIT Institute of Design in Chicago at the Illinois Institute of Technology, which was called the New Bauhaus when it opened in 1937 under the leadership of László Moholy-Nagy, and the organisation Experiments in Art and Technology (E.A.T.), which was founded by Billy Klüver, Robert Rauschenberg, Robert Whitman and Fred Waldhauer in 1966.[10] Like IHEAP, these organisations encouraged interdisciplinary collaboration.[11] With regard to structure and pedagogics, the school had some similarities with the Whitney Study Program, started under Ron Clark in New York in 1968, and with several of today's scholarship programmes and higher educations in art, critical studies and curating all over the world.[12] Theory and discussion are often essential to this type of education. The Whitney Study Program, for instance, has a model that includes a visit by a guest teacher every week and a text seminar led by the institution's professors. However, even compared to the more discursive segment of contemporary art educations, IHEAP's long days of discussions and intensive programme of guest lecturers stand out.[13]

In some sense, the Institute could be seen as an implementation of the often called-for but rarely concretised idea of art as a space for critical thinking. Students were invited to attend the Institute for a year and obtained a scholarship that was paid to them monthly. They were put in touch with the most prominent specialists in a number of fields, and all they had to do in return was to be present. No exams, no diplomas, no public exhibitions or presentations were stipulated in the final programme.[14] One obvious advantage of this structure was that it gave participants the opportunity to meet some of the most established figures on the art scene and related areas. A year at IHEAP would have provided an invaluable network. Acceptance was based partly on recommendations. The Institute

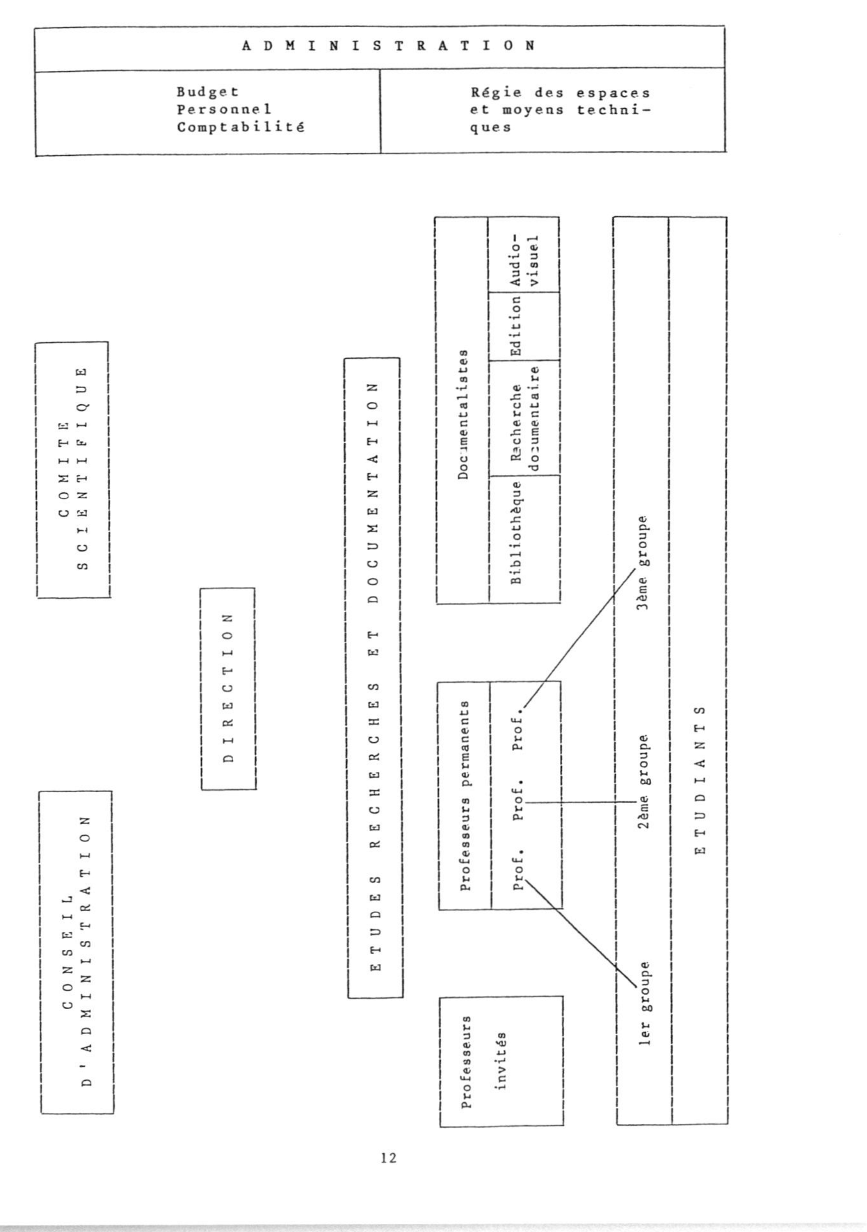

151 Organisational flowchart for Institut des Hautes Études en Arts Plastiques, Collège des Bernardins, Paris

contacted friends in prominent positions and asked them to encourage promising students to apply.[15]

Pontus Hultén planned IHEAP while working at two other institutions: as the director of the Museum of Contemporary Art (MOCA) in Los Angeles between 1981 and 1983 and the artistic director of Palazzo Grassi in Venice from 1984 to 1990. According to a note in the archive at Moderna Museet in Stockholm, Hultén had written a short resignation letter to Palazzo Grassi. In the message, written in thick felt tip in three languages (English, French and Italian), he announces that he is resigning "in order to defend the dignity of my profession".[16] The reason appears to have been a dispute regarding the institution's funding. Palazzo Grassi was financed by the Fiat motor company, and its board of directors consisted of industrialists who wanted control over its activities.[17] Donations were also the main source of MOCA's funding, a system Hultén had criticised on several occasions.[18]

Material in Moderna Museet's archives divulge that Pontus Hultén was deeply involved in the founding of IHEAP. The art school in Paris can be seen as an attempt by Hultén to return to what he considered to be the very foundation of his profession, i.e. exploring the urgent problems, in close dialogue with artists. Hultén's work at IHEAP would then be consistent with the methods he developed early on in his career as an exhibition curator. In earlier exhibitions, we have seen how Hultén tended to revisit certain issues such as movement and technology in *Movement in Art* (1961) or visions of how a future society could be organised in *Utopias and Visions* (1971). He used the material that appeared most relevant to addressing those particular issues, regardless of whether this was art or some other kind of object. Hultén was also interested in developing projects together with artists, as in *She – A Cathedral* (1966).

Within the framework of the Institute, Pontus Hultén could focus entirely on questions that interested him, in close dialogue with practising artists. In that respect, the Institute was a continuation of, or even a more radical form of, Hultén's previous work as a museum director and creator of exhibitions. IHEAP combined several of the focus areas that Hultén had explored in previous projects. The art school in Paris seems to be a place where Hultén, after years of compromising, could finally follow through on the projects he had started as a young exhibition curator. And yet, IHEAP was different in many ways from Hultén's previous field of operation. The core activity was discussions, rather than exhibitions. Moreover, IHEAP's activities were not open to the public. To achieve an open and unprestigious climate for debate, only the students, professors and invited guest lecturers had access to the Institute's discussions.[19] Journalists and the interested public were kept out. Initially, the idea was that each session would conclude with a conference, and that discussions would be published in writing in the newly-launched series *Diagonales*, published by Éditions Cercle d'Art.[20] Neither of these plans were carried out, however.[21] Excerpts from conversations in the first two years were not published in book form until 2003 and 2004.[22] Transcribing the discussions that lasted from 10 am to 6 pm three days a week for seven years proved an impossible task. Moreover, many of the voices in the tape recordings were hard to identify later.[23] Much of what was said still remains buried in the many audio tapes.[24] This could be one reason why IHEAP is still relatively unknown, compared to, say the previously-mentioned L'Académie Matisse, the Bauhaus and Black Mountain College.[25]

The Pontus Hultén Archive at Moderna Museet include five boxes of documents – programme declarations, press releases, correspondence, manuscripts for lectures, schedules and report summaries – that can provide some insights into the Institute's activities.[26] A closer scrutiny of the contents of the seven sessions held between 1988 and 1995 shows just how deeply rooted the Institute's activities were in Pontus Hultén's previous work. Under the heading of *Le Territoire de l'Art*, the Institute's first session, held in October–November 1988 and May–June 1989 under Hultén's auspices, the boundaries of art were discussed. The premise was that art in the 20th century had ceaselessly expanded its territory and had come to embrace subjects that had formerly been regarded as belonging to other disciplines, such as literature, philosophy, religion, science, economics and politics. In his programme, Hultén posits that visual arts have become a crucial medium for understanding the world.[27]

This short declaration summarises two main theses that would later permeate the Institute's entire operations. First, the discussions were based on the so-called extended concept of art, which crystallised in the 1960s and had also formed Pontus Hultén. Secondly, art was set in relation to broader social developments. Both these elements were shared by the 20th-century avant-garde, which Hultén presented, interpreted and processed throughout his career – from Kazimir Malevich's suprematism in the 1910s to the

SESSION II
Le Territoire de l'Art
"L'interprétation des oeuvres
Mise en scène, mise en espace"
20 novembre – 22 décembre 1989

JOUR	HEURE	PROGRAMME INTERVENANTS	TITRE INTERVENTIONS	PROFESSEUR
Lundi 20 novembre	9h30	Inscription des élèves	Bureau administratif 12 avenue de New York	Pontus HULTEN SARKIS Serge FAUCHEREAU
Mardi 21 novembre	9h30	a/m Séance ouverture P.HULTEN SARKIS S. FAUCHEREAU p/m SARKIS	Palais de Tokyo 2 rue de la Manutention Salle Icare	"
Mercredi 22 novembre	9h30	a/m Pontus HULTEN p/m Prés.rapide travaux élèves	Atelier Brancusi	"
Jeudi 23 novembre	9h30	Pierre CHABERT	Samuel Beckett :mise en scène: corps, lumières, noir, objets, voix	"
Vendredi 24 novembre				"
Samedi 25 novembre				"
Dimanche 26 novembre				"
Lundi 27 novembre	9h30	Serge FAUCHEREAU	Kurt Schwitters	"
rdi 28 novembre	9h30	Claude REGY	Les Espaces perdus	"
Mercredi 29 novembre	9h30	a/m discussion p/m travaux d'élèves		"
Jeudi 30 novembre	9h30	Travaux élèves		"
Vendredi 1er décembre				Sarkis absent
Samedi 2 décembre				"
Dimanche 3 décembre				"
Lundi 4 décembre	9h30	Travaux élèves/Ed RUSCHA		Pontus HULTEN Serge FAUCHEREAU SARKIS Daniel BUREN
Mardi 5 décembre	9h30	Tx élèves/At. Brancusi		
Mercredi 6 décembre	9h30	Jean-Hubert MARTIN	Marcel Broodthaers R. Filiou J. Beuys	"
Jeudi 7 décembre	9h30	Discussion Tx élèves		"
Vendredi 8 décembre				"
Samedi 9 décembre				"
manche 10 décembre				"
Lundi 11 décembre	9h30	Daniel BUREN		"
Mardi 12 décembre	9h30	Sortie : Tête Tinguely		"
Mercredi 13 décembre	9h30	Denis Bablet	Tadeusz Kantor "Espace physique espace mental	"
Jeudi 14 décembre	9h30			am P. Hulten abs. am/pm Sarkis abs.
Vendredi 15 décembre	9h30	Luciano FABRO		
Samedi 16 décembre				
Dimanche 17 décembre				
Lundi 18 décembre	9h30	Luciano BERIO	Suite à la Symphonie inachevée de Schubert	
Mardi 19 décembre	9h30	Harald SZEEMAN	Mise en espace expositions	
Mercredi 20 décembre	9h30	a/m discussion p/m travaux élèves		
Jeudi 21 décembre	9h30	Session clôture		
Vendredi 22 décembre				

Schedule for Session II Le Territoire de l'Art at Institut des Hautes Études en Arts Plastiques, Paris

institutional critique of the 1960s. Moreover, Hultén emphasised even in the programme for the first session that the purpose was not to establish a chronology; the education should not be mistaken for a course in art history, far from it ("loin de là").[28] Instead, the object was to create a situation similar to that of the studio, where each work was studied individually.[29] The art to be studied was, however, referred to in chronological order: Picasso's *Les Demoiselles d'Avignon* (1907), Duchamp's *Roue de bicyclette* (Bicycle Wheel, 1913), Malevich's *Carré noir* (Black Square, 1915), Brâncuşi's *Sculpture pour aveugles* (Sculpture for the Blind, 1925) – and it is hard not to read Hultén's ensuing lectures as initiated presentations of what is today's most canonical 20th century art history. His additions that they would also "study works by artists such as Mondrian, Matisse, Beuys, Manzoni, Klein, Francis, Tinguely, Pascali, Cornell, Kawara, Haacke, Oldenburg", and that "most of the two-month period will be devoted to art after 1945", further highlight the Institute's strong emphasis on the 20th-century art history that Hultén had outlined already in the early 1960s.[30]

The theme of the first session – the territory of art – was followed up in the second session, *Le Territoire de l'Art. L'interprétation des oeuvres. Mise en scène, mise en espace*, which was led by Sarkis in November and December 1989 and February 1990. The theme also engendered two exhibitions, one at the Russian Museum in Leningrad in May 1990, and one at the Kunst- und Ausstellungshalle der Bundesrepublik Deutschland in Bonn in 1992. These exhibitions, together with the 5,000 square-metre sculpture park at the Taejon Expo '93 in South Korea, constituted the public manifestations that were produced within the framework of IHEAP's activities.[31] The Russian Museum exhibition was preceded by a month-long sojourn in Leningrad, where the Institute's 19 students collaborated with eleven Russian artists. The mornings were devoted to discussions, with simultaneous interpretation, and the afternoons to working together in the studio that had been set up in the museum's premises.[32] The exhibition itself was in two parts, consisting of works produced by the students (an exhibition called *Ateliers*, shown in the room that had served as a studio), and a historical exhibition compiled by Hultén, *Le Territoire de l'Art, 1910–1990*.[33] The exhibition was sparsely documented, but the few photographs that do exist give the impression of a rather conventional affair, featuring some of the most famous works from the 20th century.

IHEAP opened in Paris in 1988, that is, in a milieu where discussions about the postmodern condition were running high. Jean-François Lyotard had written his report *The Postmodern Condition* already in 1979. In 1985, the exhibition *Les Immatériaux* opened at Centre Pompidou, based largely on Lyotard's analysis of the contemporary "condition".[34] In Sweden the previous year, Lars Nittve had curated the exhibition *Implosion. A Postmodern Perspective* at Moderna Museet in Stockholm, explicitly referencing Hultén's work at the Museum. In the catalogue preface, Lars Nittve writes:

> It [*Implosion*] can be seen as a natural continuation to the succession of radical exhibitions that was started as early as in the 1960s, with, for example, *4 Americans* (1962), *American Pop Art* (1964) and *Andy Warhol* (1968) and is continuing in the 1980s with *Marcel Broodthaers* (1982), *Daniel Buren* (1984) and *Vanishing Points* (1984). At the same time, the exhibition interacts in a self-evident manner with the Museum's own collections, in which the works of Marcel Duchamp and Francis Picabia, and of the American Pop artists and Minimalists, occupy a central place.[35]

When these entirely parallel manifestations are juxtaposed, it becomes clear that they represent different interpretations of 20th-century art. Whereas Hultén was still focusing on the political dimensions of the avant-garde, many expounders of postmodern art considered this to be an obsolete issue. Even the titles of the Institute sessions indicate a direction: the territory of art, the great projects, the dilemma of utopia, etcetera.[36] The aspirations on what is to be explored under these headings contrast radically with the postmodern theories and their levelling of both cultural hierarchies of value and individual agency. In an essay written for the *Implosion* catalogue, Germano Celant describes this as the death of the utopian claims of the avant-garde:

> Where the historical avant-garde dreamed of art's revolutionary power, Pop shows an art no longer capable of breaking down the process of alienation, of substituting good for bad, or revolution for capitalism; an art itself alienated, and moving within the world of commodities. Modern history attests that nothing exists outside capitalism; this is why Warhol sees the only possible existence as lying in the "disappearance of the subject", certainly the most advanced point reached in capitalism's progress, its own revolution.[37]

These formulations are entirely in line with the postmodern theories that were aired at the time, and which were perhaps most poignantly expressed in Jean Baudrillard's short essay "The Ecstasy of Communication" (first published in French in 1987). It describes not only how the relationship between the physical world and its representation collapsed, but also a short-circuiting of human agency altogether. In the final lines, the subject is described as a "switching centre for all the networks of influence", bereft of all independent agency.[38] The contrast to Pontus Hultén's faith in art and the revolutionary power of artists, as expressed in the discussions at IHEAP could hardly be more clearly articulated. Rather than engaging actively in, or even changing our way of relating to and acting in, the world, the postmodern discussions proposed an approach based on acceptance, reflection and *laissez-faire*.

Interestingly, these widely disparate interpretations of contemporary art use practically the identical set of artists and works to illustrate their historical narratives. In both versions, Marcel Duchamp is a key figure. The postmodernist expounders highlight Duchamp for having "killed" authorship, for making the distinction between original and copy irrelevant, and for having identified the work of art as an absolute fetish, i.e. devoid of essential meaning and entirely dependent on external contexts for its identity. In Hultén's interpretation, Duchamp was interesting primarily because his artistic practice was open to mechanics and movement, thereby expanding a constricted concept of art. This was why Duchamp was such a crucial eminence in Hultén's early exhibitions in the 1950s, and later in the major *Movement in Art* in 1961, which was shown in slightly different versions at Moderna Museet, the Stedelijk Museum in Amsterdam and the Louisiana Museum of Modern Art outside Copenhagen.[39]

It is this reading of Duchamp that underpins Hultén's opening lecture at IHEAP on 4 October, 1988. The focus was on how Duchamp's readymades from the 1910s had paved the way for a concept of art that embraces more than the categories of painting and sculpture, without consequently being described as a radical shift. When Hultén refers to a generation of American artists who took an interest in Duchamp in the 1950s (citing Robert Rauschenberg as his main example) he, in fact, describes how this interest has recurred throughout 20th-century art. The rendering of this central chapter in 20th-century art history, which is firmly established today, is based here on his own conversations, correspondence and exhibitions with the artists in question.[40]

Hultén's approach to postmodern theories and the artists who have come to represent them is also illustrated in the exhibition *Territorium Artis*, which was shown at Kunst- und Ausstellungshalle der Bundesrepublik Deutschland in Bonn in 1992.[41] The exhibition was not described as a product of activities at IHEAP, but there were several obvious connections. In addition to the exhibition being named after the Institute's first session, several of the Institute's professors and guest lecturers participated, and some of the artists who had been discussed in the seminars in Paris were shown.[42] The exhibition catalogue was straightforward, presenting the participating artists in alphabetical order with one or more pictures of works and a brief text. Browsing the catalogue is like seeing a medley of Hultén's previous exhibitions. In the early 1990s, Hultén's entire 40 years of mounting and creating exhibitions, networks and interpretations as a curator and museum director seems to infuse the exhibition with layers from previous exhibitions. The base consisted of *Movement in Art*, featuring Marcel Duchamp, Alexander Calder, Jean Tinguely, Naum Gabo and Man Ray.[43] From *Inner and Outer Space* we recognise artists such as Barnett Newman, Donald Judd and Yves Klein.[44] The exhibition also included American artists – Sam Francis, Jasper Johns, Claes Oldenburg, Robert Rauschenberg and Andy Warhol, along with several of those whom Hultén regularly worked with: Lucio Fontana, George Grosz, John Heartfield, Kazimir Malevich, Pablo Picasso and Niki de Saint Phalle.

To this base he added new layers: Jenny Holzer, Jeff Koons, Edward Ruscha and Jeff Wall. Altogether, Hultén's art history seems to say that 20th-century art before, after and between the two world wars was all about expanding the very concept of art. What Jenny Holzer and Jeff Koons were doing could then be interpreted as two responses to the early 20th-century avant-garde, cubism, collage, *objets trouvés* and readymades. The 1960s seem to be a bridge rather than a break between early 20th-century avant-garde and the 1980s use of everyday materials and references to popular culture. The break needed to separate postmodernism from modernism is conspicuously absent in Hultén's historiography, which seems to have remained intact since his first tentative exhibitions in the late 1950s and in the major manifestation *Movement in Art* in 1961. New artists were simply added to his established version of the history of art and its

INSTITUT DES HAUTES ETUDES
EN ARTS PLASTIQUES

mercredi, 1 avril, 1992

Cher Daniel,
j'étais très content de te voir
(si en forme) hier.

Merci pour ta promesse de faire
un texte pour: A R T.

Le catalogue est très avancé.
Le plus tôt possible serait
très apprecié.

bien à toi
ton
Pontus

HÔTEL DE SAINT-AIGNAN - ANNEXE
75, rue du Temple 75003 Paris
Téléphone : (1) 48 87 05 00 Télécopie : (1) 48 87 03 88
ASSOCIATION RÉGIE PAR LA LOI DE 1901

Letter from Pontus Hultén to Daniel Buren, 1 April, 1992

position in society. Hultén had become his own encyclopaedia, built on personal contacts and memories from the 20th-century art history that was entirely uncontested at the time. An impartial reading of Hultén's version of 20th-century art history could open for a more nuanced perception of the postmodern in relation to the modern. Rather than disputes and breaks, it reveals repetitions of methods and gestures, and persistent work on a set of recurring problems.

1. According to a description of how IHEAP came about, "Chronologie de l'évolution: 'L'ÉCOLE DE PARIS'", Chirac allegedly proposed that Hultén should start the school during a meeting with Mme Georges Pompidou (Claude Jacqueline Pompidou). The document is undated, but it states that at the time of writing, the school was planned to open in 1985. MMA PHA 4.3.2. In Annick Boisnard's article it is however stated that Chirac gave this assignment to Hultén in 1983, see "Présentation de l'Institut des Hautes Études en Arts Plastiques. Novembre 1985–Décembre 1995", *Quand les artistes font école. Vingt-quatre journées de l'Institut des Hautes Études en Arts Plastiques 1988–1990, Tome I*, eds. Marie-Sophie Boulan, Paris: Amis de l'Institut des Hautes Études en Arts Plastiques and Éditions du Centre Pompidou, 2003, p. 21.

2. The Institute was initially financed by the City of Paris, a private donor, the Ministry of Culture, Communication, and Major Projects Relating to the Bicentennial ("le Ministère de la Culture, de la Communication, des Grands Travaux et de Bicentenaire"), press release, 30 November, 1988. MMA PHA 4.3.2.

3. Daniel Buren, "Témoignage", *Quand les artistes font école, Tome I*, 2003, p. 19, which can be compared to the forward-looking document "Concept et organisation", where it appears that the plan was to invite four guest professors for a period of two years, and that they, in turn, could invite relevant guest lecturers. See "Institut des Hautes Études en Arts Plastiques. Collège des Bernardins. Concept et organisation", p. 5, undated, but similar to the document dated February 1987. Verksamhet 2. MMA PHA 4.3.2.

4. The students' board and lodging were covered by an annual grant paid monthly. "Institut des Hautes Études en Arts Plastiques. Collège des Bernardins. Concept et organisation", p. 6. MMA PHA 4.3.2.

5. "Institut des Hautes Études en Arts Plastiques. Collège des Bernardins. Concept et organisation", pp. 1–2. MMA PHA 4.3.2.

6. In the plans, this was formulated as: "lieux où se réalisait la transmission du savoir et de l'expérience"; see, for example, the aforementioned "Institut des Hautes Études en Arts Plastiques. Collège des Bernardins. Concept et organisation", p. 1. MMA PHA 4.3.2.

7. "Institut des Hautes Études en Arts Plastiques. Collège des Bernardins. Concept et organisation", p. 2. MMA PHA 4.3.2. Original text: "Partant de l'axiome qu'avant d'être un technicien, un professionnel habile, l'artiste est quelqu'un qui réfléchit et se sent concerné par le monde et la vie, les études proposées à l'institut veulent privilégier l'être sans préjudice du faire." *L'être* and *faire* is underlined in the original text. See also Marie-Françoise Rousseau, "L'Institut des Hautes Études en Arts Plastiques. Point d'orgue du Centre Pompidou", *Les Cahiers du Musée national d'art moderne*, Paris: Éditions du Centre George Pompidou, no. 141, autumn 2017, p. 100.

8. See press release, 30 November, 1988. MMA PHA 4.3.2. See also statements such as these: "Une très grande importance est donnée aux échange conviviaux entre professeurs et élèves qui ont lieu notamment lors des repas en commun et des reunions informelles", in "Institut des Hautes Études

en Arts Plastiques. Collège des Bernardins. Concept et organisation", p. 3. MMA PHA 4.3.2.

9. Unlike them, however, they wanted IHEAP to focus less on teaching artistic techniques, and more on preparing students for "la grande richesse de notre culture contemporaine". "Institut des Hautes Études en Arts Plastiques. Collège des Bernardins. Concept et organisation", p. 1. MMA PHA 4.3.2. Pontus Hultén is also said to have hesitated to use the term *art school*, since it suggested a more conventional pedagogy. Instead of pupils or students, the young artists were referred to as "artistes-boursiers". Marie-Françoise Rousseau, "L'Institut des Hautes Études en Arts Plastiques. Point d'orgue du Centre Pompidou", *Les Cahiers*, 2017, pp. 100–101

10. See *Teknologi för livet. Om Experiments in Art and Technology*, Paris: Schultz Förlag AB and Norrköping: Norrköpings Konsemuseum, 2004, and Marianne Hultman, "Our Man in New York. An Interview with Billy Klüver on His Collaboration with Moderna Museet", *The History Book. On Moderna Museet 1958–2008,* eds. Anna Tellgren and Martin Sundberg, Stockholm: Moderna Museet and Göttingen: Steidl, 2008, pp. 235–256.

11. Marie-Françoise Rousseau, "L'Institut des Hautes Études en Arts Plastiques. Point d'orgue du Centre Pompidou", *Les Cahiers*, 2017, p. 99.

12. Ibid., p. 100. See also *Independent Study Program. 40 Years Whitney Museum of American Art 1968–2008*, ed. Margaret Liu Clinton, New York: Whitney Museum of American Art, 2008.

13. "The Independent Study Program 1968–2008", *Independent Study Program. 40 Years. Whitney Museum of American Art 1968–2008*, 2008, p. 12, author unnamed. See also the description of the scholars ("les boursiers") in "Institut des Hautes Études en Arts Plastiques. Collège des Bernardins. Concept et organisation", p. 6. MMA PHA 4.3.2.

14. "Institut des Hautes Études en Arts Plastiques. Collège des Bernardins. Concept et organisation", pp. 6–7. MMA PHA 4.3.2.

15. Viveka Rinman, *Institut des Hautes Études en Arts Plastiques. Pontus Hulténs internationella konstskola i Paris 1988–1995*, BA paper (60 points) Department of Art History, Stockholm: Stockholm University, 1998, p. 17. Based on the material in Moderna Museet's archives, it would be interesting to study the networks. Most of the invited guest lecturers were born in the 1930s and 1940s, whereas the artist/students were born in the 1960s. The Institute can be seen as one generation passing the baton on to the next. This generational change is also specific to the Swedish context, as pointed out in *Pontus Hultén på Moderna Moderna Museet. Vittnesseminarium, Södertörns högskola, 26 april 2017*, eds. Charlotte Bydler, Andreas Gedin and Johanna Ringarp, Samtidshistoriska frågor 38, Huddinge: Södertörn University, 2018.

16. Undated note by Pontus Hultén. MMA PHA 4.1.49.

17. "Pontus Hultén Directeur Artistique du Palazzo Grassi à Venise, Directeur de l'Institut des Hautes Études en Arts Plastiques à Paris", 3 April, 1987. MMA PHA 4.3.2.

18. See Pontus Hultén, "Sandberg och Stedelijk Museum", *Stedelijk Museum, Amsterdam besöker Moderna Museet, Stockholm*, ed. K. G. Hultén,

Moderna Museet exhibition catalogue no. 19, Stockholm: Moderna Museet, 1962, p. 5. Hultén repeats his criticism more than thirty years later in a letter to Claes Oldenburg and Coosje van Bruggen, 1 June, 1999. MMA PHA 5.1.28.

19. Viveka Rinman, *Institut des Hautes Études en Arts Plastiques*, 1998, p. 27.

20. "Institut des Hautes Études en Arts Plastiques. Collège des Bernardins. Concept et organisation", pp. 5–6. MMA PHA 4.3.2.

21. Viveka Rinman, *Institut des Hautes Études en Arts Plastiques*, 1998, p. 42.

22. See *Quand les artistes font école. Vingt-quatre journées de l'Institut des Hautes Études en Arts Plastiques 1988–1990, Tome I*, ed. Marie-Sophie Boulan, Paris: Amis de l'Institut des Hautes Études en Arts Plastiques, 2003, and *Quand les artistes font école. Vingt-quatre journées de l'Institut des Hautes Études en Arts Plastiques 1991–1992, Tome II*, ed. Marie-Sophie Boulan, Paris: Amis de l'Institut des Hautes Études en Arts Plastiques, 2004.

23. Viveka Rinman, *Institut des Hautes Études en Arts Plastiques*, 1998, p. 27.

24. In 1996, these tapes and the Institute's library were donated to Galeries Contemporaines des Musées de Marseilles, which had opened two years earlier. Marie-Sophie Boulan was in charge of building its library between 1994 and 1997. Danièle Giraudy, "Avant-Propose", *Quand les artistes font école, Tome I*, 2003, p. 5.

25. Viveka Rinman wrote a BA dissertation in Art History in 1998 about IHEAP, based largely on interviews with participants, including Hultén and the permanent professors and administration staff. Rinman also interviewed the Swedish artists that were at the Institute at various times, Anna Selander, Jan Svenungsson and Sophie Tottie. This dissertation is still an important basic research source in the field. See Viveka Rinman, *Institut des Hautes Études en Arts Plastiques,* 1998.

26. See MMA PHA 4.3.1–5.

27. See Session 1 "Le Territoire de l'Art", undated document. MMA PHA 4.3.2.

28. Ibid.

29. Hultén writes: "l'intention n'étant pas de faire un cours d'histoire de l'art mais de créer une situation d'atelier où chaque œuvre d'art sera étudiée individuellment", in "Le Territoire de l'Art". MMA PHA 4.3.2.

30. In Hultén's original French: "On examine aussi par example, des œuvres de Mondrian, Matisse, Beuys, Manzoni, Klein, Francis, Tinguely, Pascali, Cornell, Kawara, Haacke, Oldenburg. La majeure partie des deux mois sera donc consacrée à l'art après 1945.", in "Le Territoire de l'Art", undated document. MMA PHA 4.3.2. For Hultén's interpretation of 20th-century art in the exhibition *Movement in Art* (1961), see also Anna Lundström, "Movement in Art. The Layers of an Exhibition", *Pontus Hultén and Moderna Museet. The Formative Years,* eds. Anna Tellgren and Anna Lundström, Stockholm: Moderna Museet and London: Koenig Books, 2017, pp. 67–93.

31. The sculpture park was part of the major science and technology expo in Taejon in 1993. Pontus Hultén was invited by the South Korean

government in 1992 and commissioned to organise a 5,000-square-metre sculpture park in the middle of the exhibition grounds. The South Korean government earmarked 20 million French francs for the project. See Viveka Rinman, *Institut des Hautes Études en Arts Plastiques*, 1998, pp. 35–36.

32. Ibid., pp. 31–32.

33. The study trip to Leningrad, and IHEAP in general, were funded mainly by the City of Paris and the Ministry of Culture in Paris, the Getty Grant Program, Los Angeles, and Cartier International, Paris. "Institut des Hautes Études en Arts Plastiques", October, 1987. MMA PHA 4.3.2. See also Annick Boisnard, "Présentation de l'Institut des Hautes Études en Arts Plastiques", *Quand les artistes font école, Tome I*, 2003, p. 24. Additional funding for the exhibition at the Russian Museum in Leningrad was provided by the Soviet Ministry of Culture and Canal+ in France. Viveka Rinman, *Institut des Hautes Études en Arts Plastiques*, 1998, pp. 31–32.

34. Jean-François Lyotard and Thierry Chaput co-curated the exhibition, in collaboration with a larger team. For more on the exhibition, see *30 Years after Les Immatériaux*, eds. Yuk Hui and Andreas Broeckmann, Lüneburg: Meson Press, 2015, and John Rajchman, "*Les Immatériaux* or How to Construct the History of Exhibitions", *Tate Papers. Landmark Exhibitions Issue,* no. 12, 2009, https://www.tate.org.uk/research/tatepapers/12/les-immateriaux-or-how-to-construct-the-history-of-exhibitions (23 August, 2022).

35. Lars Nittve, "Preface", *Implosion. A Postmodern Perspective*, eds. Lars Nittve and Margareta Helleberg, Moderna Museet exhibition catalogue no. 217, Stockholm: Moderna Museet, 1987, p. 9.

36. As mentioned previously, classes consisted mainly on seminar-like discussion. They related to given themes that were pursued throughout the academic year, so-called sessions. The session titles in French were in chronological order: *Le Territoire de l'Art*, *La Situation de l'artiste*, *Les Grands Projets*, *Y a-t-il recherche dans l'art*, *Le centre et la périphérie*, *De l'abri à l'utopie et vice versa*.

37. Germano Celant, "Subject in Short Circuit", *Implosion*, 1987, p. 174.

38. English translation from Jean Baudrillard, "The Ecstasy of Communication", transl. John Johnston, *The Anti-Aesthetic. Essays on Postmodern Culture*, ed. Hal Foster, New York: The New Press, 1998, p. 153. The text was first published in *L'autre par lui-même*, Paris: Éditions Galilée, 1987. It is interesting to compare this with IHEAP's explicit intention to resume the link to the ambitions of the avant-garde. See, for instance, how Marie-Françoise Rousseau expresses this: "La conception inédit de cette nouvelle 'école d'art' se cristallisait autour de la transmission de l'esprit des avant-gardes, laquelle s'exprima dans la structure, le recrutement, le fonctionnement et les démarches de l'Institut." See in Marie-Françoise Rousseau, "L'Institut des Hautes Études en Arts Plastiques. Point d'orgue du Centre Pompidou", *Les Cahiers*, 2017, p. 101.

39. See the aforementioned Anna Lundström, "Movement in Art. The Layers of an Exhibition", Pontus Hultén and Moderna Museet. The Formative Years, 2017, pp. 67–93, and Anna Lundström, "Marcel Duchamp via

Pontus Hultén", https://www.modernamuseet.se/stockholm/sv/utstallningar/picassoduchamp/marcel-duchamp-via-pontus-hulten (23 August, 2022), produced in conjunction with the exhibition Picasso/Duchamp "He Was Wrong", featured at Moderna Museet in 2012.

40. Marcel Duchamp's influence on the art concept that emerged in the 1950s in general and on the younger generation of American artists in particular has been profusely researched. For an in-depth study of the change of generations, see, for instance, *Dancing around the Bride. Cage, Cunningham, Johns, Rauschenberg, and Duchamp* (exh. cat.), ed. Carlos Basualdo, New Haven: Yale University Press, 2013. For Duchamp's relationship to the Swedish art scene, see the documentation of the symposium *Duchamp and Sweden. On the Reception of Marcel Duchamp after World War II* at Moderna Museet in Stockholm, 28–30 April, 2015, https://www.modernamuseet.se/stockholm/en/event/symposium-duchamp-and-sweden/ (23 August, 2022).

41. See *Territorium Artis* (exh. cat.), ed. Pontus Hultén, Bonn: Kunst- und Ausstellungshalle der Bundesrepublik Deutschland, 1992. Hultén was the artistic director of Kunst- und Ausstellungshalle der Bundesrepublik Deutschland in Bonn from 1990 to 1995.

42. One example is Hans Haacke who was guest lecturer at the Institute on 10 October, 1988, and based his lecture "Esthétique et architecture" on his work *Oil Painting. Hommage à Marcel Broodthaers* (1982). See *Quand les artistes font école, Tome I*, 2003, pp. 55–91. Another example is Pontus Hultén who based his lecture on the 15 October, 1991, "Constantin Brâncuşi, Le Parc de Tîrgu Jiu et L'Atelier", on Brâncuşi's studio, which was reconstructed to be built near Centre Pompidou. See *Quand les artistes font école, Tome II*, 2004, pp. 589–617.

43. A letter from Hultén to Duchamp, dated 1 December, 1954, concerning a radio programme on Dada he was working on, and which Duchamp returned with notes in the margin, was photographed and reproduced in the catalogue *Territorium Artis,* 1992, p. 72. The letter is a distinct example of how Hultén had certainly become his own history book by that time. The letter is now in The Pontus Hultén Archive at Moderna Museet. MMA PHA 5.1.10.

44. For an analysis of *The Inner and Outer Space*, see Patrik Andersson, "The Inner and Outer Space. Rethinking Movement in Art", *Pontus Hultén and Moderna Museet. The Formative Years,* 2017, pp. 39–63.

TOWARDS A MUSEUM OF THE FUTURE

opus

24/25

15 F INTERNATIONAL

Cover of *Opus International,* nos. 24–25, 1971

Towards a Museum of the Future. Interview with Pontus Hultén

Yann Pavie

Opus International *was a French journal for contemporary art (1967–1995) that covered and commented on new tendencies in art in three issues per year. The collective of art critics that wrote for the journal included Alain Jouffroy, Jean-Clarence Lambert and Anne Tronche. Yann Pavie, an art critic since the late 1960s, was a curator at ARC (Animation – Recherche – Confrontation) at the Musée d'art moderne de la ville de Paris between 1973 and 1976. The interview with Pontus Hultén is part of a theme in the journal "Vers le musée du futur" (Towards the Museum of the Future). In his introduction, Pavie refers to the fundamental issue of the role of museums in society and the social purpose of art. He mentions a few European initiatives he finds interesting, one of which is Peter F. Althaus's project "Le musée ouvert" (The Open Museum) at the Kunsthalle in Basel, and another is Pontus Hultén's activities at Moderna Museet in Stockholm. The model with four circles that Hultén used to describe the museum of the future is the most acknowledged in recent times of these initiatives. Hultén's ideas were formulated in discussions with Pär Stolpe and others, in connection with the plans to relocate Moderna Museet to Kulturhuset in central Stockholm.*

OPUS: How would you define the role and function of a modern art museum?

PONTUS HULTÉN: Your question actually raises the problem of the future of such a museum, or that of the "museum of the future". It is with this in mind that we have set out to analyse the roles, functions, and structures of our museum.

Until 1960 museums were based on the same conceptions informing the 19th-century museum. Nothing had fundamentally changed, other than the fact that the focus was on modern objects.

This was a "museum for visits", dedicated to the worship of objects. In around 1960, we discovered that in a museum of this kind, things could be shown and done that society did not accept elsewhere: "works of art" that were inadmissible anywhere but in such a space … We have attempted to expand this conception. We have played music that couldn't be played in concert halls, screened films that couldn't be projected in movie theatres … The space became a *Cour des Miracles*, a place where society tolerated acts that were out of the ordinary. This situation was recognised by artists, musicians, filmmakers, museum professionals and so on, as much abroad as in Sweden.

But, in my opinion, this situation lasted only from 1960 to 1968. In 1968, as a result of the events in May, it could not continue because it would have it lent itself to the idea that the modern art museum was simply a *Cour des Miracles*, a closed, isolated place where everything was permissible because there were no repercussions on social reality.

We came to realise that events in the street had a more powerful creative force. Thus, we have to prove that the actions and objects in our intuitions can serve as examples for all the activities that renew people's mentalities. We have to demonstrate that our events and activities, at their own level and with their own means of existence, have value as a reality and can thereby inspire a new conception of life.

OPUS: On what elements, from this perspective, does your analysis focus? No doubt, four could probably be identified: contemporary art, the museum as such, the public and the notion of a society's culture.

P.H.: We started from the last point and tried to see the role the museum could have in the public arena. During the days of May 1968, the prevailing mentality, the state of mind was informed by spontaneity. Our objective is to ensure that ideas that expand the conception of life find a place where they can be expressed and developed in a permanent way.

We asked ourselves if it would be possible to hold onto the essence of the May 1968 situation, the "situation in the streets" where everyone was out there, regardless of class and without necessarily having a particularly "cultivated attitude", without feeling rejected.

We started with this question to build up a theoretical model for a modern museum. We imagined an abstract three-dimensional model, spherical in appearance. The sphere comprises four concentric layers.

The outer layer, the spherical envelope, that corresponds to the universe of daily life, is characterised by an accelerated concentration of information. This information must be filtered as little as possible. The materials for us in this layer are raw and direct. There will be, for example, tickers from all the news agencies.

This will represent a sort of "degree zero" of information, a place where the individual is assaulted by information of all sorts. Obviously it is impossible to obtain non-manipulated information, but the very fact that the information will often be contradictory will create a conflictual situation, one that lends itself to critique. The situation in the streets is thereby recreated and intensified, and the conditions for discussion are enhanced.

The second layer will be devoted to workshops. It will provide spaces where tools and other means of production will be made available: from hammers and nails to brushes and computers. The tools are provided but nothing is decided as to their use, the fields to be exploited, or the aims of experimentation. The museum staff could serve as instructors for these machines. These workshops could be used by a single artist, a group of artists, by us, by anyone. Specialists in the field of art or communication will work there on all types of problems.

The third layer of the sphere will present the productions from the workshops and will be dedicated to events: visual arts, films, photographs, dance, concerts, but also exhibition of ready-made products. While the area is dedicated to recognised cultural activities, the contacts with the workshops will endow them with a more revolutionary dimension.

The last layer, the core, will contain the memory of the information processed. This is the museum's role of preservation and collection.

OPUS: This latter function, it would seem, is open to debate.

P.H.: True. There are differences of opinion among curators on this issue. As far as I'm concerned, I have a positive response to this. Collecting must remain, even if this poses practical problems regarding the works that we have a historical responsibility to conserve. These would be works we decided to keep as testimony to the events we organise, but they could also be elements, such as artworks, films, and tapes, acquired elsewhere …

In my opinion, the collection represents a necessary continuity. Collective memory is important and the image seems to me to be one of the most concentrated forms of human experience that can be consulted.

One last point: an institution like ours is quite vulnerable to the reactionary forces of society. The collection can be a safeguard, the guarantor of the trace left by the passage of people at a given point in time. Let's not forget the thirties in Germany …

OPUS: That said, you are announcing innovations?

P.H.: What's new is the addition of the two first layers that connect the museum institution to the social phenomena of everyday life, in which it thereby participate directly – a critical participation with all that we can bring to it that is upbeat, joyful and a little bit more insane.

Our theoretical model is based on a complete communication in both directions, not only between the concentric layers but also between the outside world, the public arena, and the inside, the museum.

We also need to devise a permanent system of transmissions between the different layers, not only within the institution, but also with all institutions of the same type and with a variety of dissemination and communication organisations: newspapers and audiovisual media …

The purpose of all this is not to monopolise a certain category of information but rather to increase in number the sources of information.

OPUS: Practically speaking, do you imagine having distinctive spaces designed based on the different functions that you have attributed to the "museum of the future"?

P.H.: As a basic principle, in the building that we are having constructed, there will not be permanent partitions between the areas that could be used as workshops for artists, the public or ourselves. This allows for free communication on all levels and facilitates exchanges of ideas at all times. But if ever someone is working on a long project, it would certainly be possible to isolate that person. This design solution is incidentally more practical insofar as museum surveillance is concerned.

Ballet Cunningham : Happening « 5 soirées New-Yorkaises », Moderna Museet, Stockholm, 1964

Traiter de la muséographie contemporaine, c'est poser la question du rôle et de la fonction du musée dans notre société. C'est d'emblée poser le problème de la fonction sociale de l'art et celui du besoin culturel de cette société.

Le fait est connu qu'il existe un décalage d'au moins cinquante ans entre la création des idées — innovation inéluctable — et leur acceptation par le grand public. Il ne serait sans doute pas exagéré de dire que « l'œuvre d'art » reconnue comme telle, s'arrête à la représentation de portrait, paysage ou nature morte. Aujourd'hui encore, le seul enseignement donnant droit au diplôme de professorat de dessin et d'histoire de l'art, ne fait que renforcer ces idées reçues : le dessin d'après l'antique, le modèle vivant ou la nature morte sont de rigueur ; on plante encore son chevalet dans les salles du Louvre. On comprend pourquoi Cézanne fut l'objet de tant de scandale, lui qui osa peindre la figure humaine comme une simple pomme : ravaler la « dignité » humaine au rang de l'objet défie la morale humaniste, puritaine, pour qui une sorte de nature majuscule est le décor des faits et gestes de l'homme avec tout ce que ce concept peut impliquer d'absolu. Devant le portrait d'Ambroise Vollard, on a envie de parler peinture et non fonction sociale ou intensité psychologique comme on le ferait devant un portrait de David.

Voilà le drame de la soi-disant compréhension de l'objet appelé « œuvre d'art », d'autant que cette reconnaissance, avant d'être dictée par les significations propres de l'œuvre, est décrétée par sa cote marchande, seul garant d'une « Beauté » dont la fonction essentielle est de soutenir le prestige d'une classe privilégiée. L'art ne devient plus qu'un objet et n'est plus considéré que par rapport au système global de consommation des objets. Ainsi, le critère de distinction de tel ou tel artiste obéit aux fluctuations de la mode, aux facéties des valeurs boursières, selon le mouvement perpétuel du processus production/consommation à un certain prix, caution d'une bonne qualité. Système rassurant que de bloquer le discours des idées par une telle surenchère ! Le marché de l'art est ainsi fait.

A ce premier stade se situe le rôle de la galerie-marchande de tableaux pour le moderne, celui de l'expert et du commissaire-priseur pour l'ancien.

Intervient ensuite le musée, dont la fonction est de conserver et d'augmenter tant bien que mal le patrimoine artistique de la nation, un de ses plus beaux fleurons pour une politique culturelle de prestige. Il sanctifie l'heureux élu par de pompeuses rétrospectives d'objets authentiques, uniques, rares et, par conséquent, « beaux ». L'artiste obtient enfin le droit de pénétrer dans ce « Saint des Saints », et ainsi, de recueillir la récompense suprême : l'adulation et la reconnaissance éternelle.

Cette image de marque « œuvre d'art » est, de plus, largement diffusée par les mass-média, illusion d'une culture de masse universelle, qui comme le remarque Baudrillard, « parle à tous pour mieux remettre chacun à sa place », pour renforcer sous couleur de l'abolir « l'inégalité culturelle et la discrimination sociale ». Curieusement, ce sont elles qui, aujourd'hui, propagent l'idéologie humaniste (je regarde vivre en me regardant vivre) et sanctionnent la compréhension de « l'œuvre d'art » selon des valeurs idéalistes, symboliques et hiérarchisées. Au nom de cette morale, l'art contemporain n'est-il pas repertorié sous les étiquettes « anti-esthétique » ou « anti-art » ?

Ces indices critiques, multiples facettes d'une même réalité, sont autant de points de conflit qu'ils déterminent les orientations actuelles des sciences humaines et de l'activité artistique. Cette évolution des idées fait valoir une volonté de combler le vide entre « art » et « vie », « théorie » et « pratique », « culture cultivée » et « culture de masse ». Ce faisant, elle a pour impératif l'essor d'une nouvelle idée de culture qui est une ré-flexion en tant que mise en situation des données précédentes désormais conçues comme ensemble relatif d'informations, et non plus comme processus accumulatif de points de repère, expression d'un savoir dont l'universalité serait cautionnée par son modèle théorique : la vie de l'homme (naissance, maturité/apogée, déclin/décadence). En puisant ses thèmes dans les réalités du quotidien en lui empruntant ses « mises en page », ses techniques d'expression, l'art contemporain ne devient plus qu'information et n'est plus que création et recherche active sur les moyens permettant la mise en relation des diverses informations du réel. Cette culture à l'état naissant, avec tout ce qu'elle comporte de paradoxes et de contradictions dans la mesure où elle est directement confrontée avec le quotidien, demande l'établissement de centres de diffusion, nouveau statut de l'institution/musée en tant qu'institut de recherche et fondation de créativité.

Dans cette perspective, depuis une quinzaine d'années, des initiatives intéressantes ont vu le jour afin de concréter ce nouvel état d'esprit : celles de E. de Wilde au Stedelijk Museum d'Amsterdam, de K.G. Pontus Hulten au Moderna Museet de Stockholm, de Pierre Gaudibert à l'A.R.C., de H. Szeeman en Suisse, de M. Kustow en Angleterre, de Duncan F. Cameron au Canada... Récemment, vient de se tenir à la Kunsthalle de Bâle, une manifestation qui, sous le titre **Le musée ouvert**, présentait un travail collectif dirigé par le conservateur de ce musée, Peter Althaus. Ce projet part de l'idée que le musée, en tant que moyen de cohésion de la communauté urbaine, doit être repensé en termes d'instrument de diffusion active et de communication permanente. La conception de ce « musée du futur » procédait d'études plus générales sur les espaces urbains et sur les systèmes de construction rationnels. Cette exposition, en effet, insistait sur le fait que l'efficacité de la fonction de ce musée ouvert qui renvoie réciproquement à l'idée d'une « ville ouverte » dépendait avant tout de ses structures architectoniques en liaison avec un projet d'urbanisme de la cité tout entière.

Voilà brièvement posés quelques problèmes concernant la réalité culturelle de notre société, problèmes complexes car liés à la réalité économique et sociale. Aujourd'hui ces questions prêtent à controverse car elles sont mal assimilées, ou jugées utopiques, ou encore sont dites subversives. Nous les avons soumises (au seuil d'une vaste enquête qui se répercutera de numéro en numéro) à plusieurs conservateurs qui incarnent l'évolution de cette nouvelle activité culturelle, activité qui, nous le pensons, présidera aux orientations futures de l'histoire de l'art. Nous publions aujourd'hui la réponse de Pontus Hulten, conservateur du Moderna Museet de Stockholm. ■

57

Exposition « Le Modèle », 1968

la communication y travailleront sur toutes sortes de problèmes.

La troisième couche de la sphère, présentera les productions des ateliers et sera consacrée aux manifestations : arts plastiques, films, photos, danse, concerts... mais aussi les expositions des « produits tout faits ». Il s'agit ici de l'activité culturelle déjà connue. Mais il semble que les contacts avec les ateliers donneront à cette activité un aspect plus révolutionnaire.

La dernière couche, le noyau, comprendra la « mémoire » des informations traitées ; c'est le rôle de conservation et de collection du musée.

Opus : **Il semblerait que cette dernière fonction soit discutée ?**

P. H. : **En effet, cette question occasionne certaines divergences parmi les conservateurs des musées d'art moderne. En ce qui me concerne, j'y réponds positivement. La collection doit rester, même si cela pose des problèmes d'ordre pratique quant à la conservation des œuvres qui incombent une responsabilité historique. Ce sera ce que l'on a décidé de garder en tant que témoignage de nos manifestations ; ce peut être également des éléments que l'on se procure ailleurs : œuvres, films, bandes magnétiques... A mon avis, cette collection représente une continuité nécessaire. La mémoire collective est importante en ce sens que l'image me semble être une des formes les plus concentrées du vécu des expériences humaines que l'on peut consulter.**

Un dernier point encore ; une institution comme la nôtre est assez vulnérable aux forces réactionnaires de la société. La collection, ce peut être un « sauf-conduit », le garant de la trace laissée par le passage de l'homme à une certaine époque donnée. Rappelons-nous les années trente en Allemagne...

Opus : **Ceci dit, vous annoncez des innovations ?**

P. H. : **La nouveauté, c'est l'addition des deux premières couches qui relient et font participer directement l'institution-musée aux phénomènes sociaux de la vie quotidienne, participation critique avec tout ce que nous pouvons y apporter de gai, de joyeux et d'un peu plus fou.**

Notre modèle théorique imagine une communication complète dans les deux sens, non seulement entre les couches concentriques, mais encore entre le monde du dehors, la cité, et le monde du dedans, le musée.

Il faut aussi envisager un système permanent d'émissions entre les diverses couches, non seulement à l'intérieur de l'institution, mais encore avec toutes les institutions du même genre, et avec les organismes de diffusion et de communication : presse écrite et parlée... Le but de tout cela n'est pas tant de monopoliser une certaine catégorie d'informations que de multiplier les sources d'information.

Opus : **Pratiquement, envisagez-vous**

1958 1959 1960 1961 1962 1963 1964 1965 1966 1967 1968 1969

VISITES COMMENTEES ET CONFERENCES POUR ENFANTS...

VISITES COMMENTEES ET CONFERENCES POUR ADULTES

LE MODERNA MUSEET : NOMBRE DE VISITEURS

61

Opus International, nos. 24–25, 1971, pp. 56–57, 60–61

OPUS: Museum surveillance is a thorny problem. Have you found an original way to resolve it?

P.H.: We prefer thinking of the surveillance staff as monitors rather than guards, because they are there not only to guard the tools, but also to inform the public. Obviously, a repressive, policing attitude on the part of the staff must be avoided. At the Moderna Museet, this personnel is strictly female: they are what could be called "hostesses", though I don't love the word. By their role which is essentially to inform and instruct the public, these new "guards" have responsibilities towards the public and in this way they participate in the life of the museum.

OPUS: The "education" of the public seems to be one of the major obstacles that could ruin the usefulness of contemporary art museums. Should such a museum take into consideration the population regardless of class or should it continue to address an elite, choice public? How can you manage to interest as many people as possible?

P.H.: This, to my mind, is not the real issue, since the museum alone cannot be expected to resolve this most important problem. I can offer a reply based on two observations. When a worker comes to repair the roof or the piping, in other words when he comes to the museum for a professional reason, he is usually interested (when he's being paid, of course). But the idea of walking into the museum on his own initiative for leisure purposes would surely not occur to him. Each class has its own "cultural attitudes" and "practices" that are strongly bound up with its conventions and ethos. This cultural structure will not change until classes in society break down. As things stand right now, we can only hope at best to contribute to this change. We must trust in artistic activity as the subtlest and at the same time the most incisive means of expression.

OPUS: In that case, is the solution purely political?

P.H.: I don't believe that it is purely political insofar as the worker will hold on to the same cultural attitude dictated by the morality of the class to which he belongs, even if he steps into a managerial position in his business.

OPUS: Yes, but everything is connected. I mean that political and economic thinking, social attitudes and artistic production form a coherent whole in the history of society. For example, the art market maintains a warped relationship to the artwork and to the function of the museum by providing them with a specific brand image: an object of speculation and a temple of universal knowledge dedicated to the cult of the "valuable" object …

P.H.: In that sense, it is political. But I'd like to add that since around 1960, the modern art museum has no longer been considered a temple of culture with a capital C. This idea seems outdated to me. The difficulty resides in the fact that we have to promote the modern art museum as a haven of freedom, perhaps the only one that can exist among institutions.

This can only be achieved by way of a profound change in the global structures of our society, a shift toward a so-called civilisation of leisure.

OPUS: And what about galleries? What about the art market? How does Moderna Museet fit into this market?

P.H.: With our mode of society being what it is, we cannot ask artists to be beggars.

Galleries are useful, but it seems to me that the commercialisation of art has been driven to extremes since 1960. Galleries have gone too far and this is dangerous.

Sellers and artists have been corrupted by the enormous ease of a "consumer society" that regards the art object as a product of speculation and nothing more.

It is, of course, impossible for us to put a stop to such a system. Actually we have tried to do what we could to encourage purchases directly from the artists instead of through the galleries, with artists coming to propose their works, to leave them or images of them, in the museum. In that way, our museum becomes like an open square where artists and the public meet each other in a healthier way. This extra role, which is necessary to my mind, creates a new, parallel and complementary situation that makes it possible to escape a warped pricing system, one that does not correspond in the least to the reality of the visual arts.

entretien avec pontus hulten

HULTEN,
Karl Gunnar Pontus Vougt
né le 21-6-1924
1945-50
Etudes d'histoire de l'art
et d'ethnographie
à l'université de Stockholm
1950-55
Etudes à Stockholm
et à Paris ;
journalisme et cinéma
1957
Conservateur assistant
au musée d'art moderne
de Stockholm
1960
Premier conservateur
du nouveau Moderna Museet
1961
Exposition :
« Art en mouvement »
1964
Collabore à l'exposition
« Le musée de nos désirs »
1966
Exposition :
« Monde intérieur
et monde extérieur »
1968
Exposition :
« La machine »
1969
Refuse en tant que
commissaire pour la Suède
de participer à la Biennale
de Sao-Paulo
1970
« Alternative Suédoise »

Opus : **Comment définissez-vous le rôle et la fonction d'un musée d'art moderne ?**

Pontus Hulten : **Cette question pose en fait le problème de l'avenir d'un tel musée, ou celle du « musée de l'avenir ». A ce propos, nous avons essayé d'analyser les rôles, fonctions et structures de notre musée.**

Avant 1960, celui-ci était fondé sur les mêmes conceptions que l'était un musée au XIXe siècle. Rien n'était au fond changé, si ce n'est qu'on s'occupait d'objets modernes.

C'est le « musée-visite » consacré au culte des objets. Autour de 1960, on a découvert que, dans ce genre de musée, on pouvait montrer des choses et réaliser des actes que la société n'acceptait pas ailleurs : des « œuvres d'art » inadmissibles, sauf en cet endroit précis... Nous avons essayé d'élargir cette conception. On jouait de la musique qui ne pouvait pas être jouée dans les salles de concert, on présentait des films qui ne pouvaient pas être projetés dans les salles de spectacles... Ce lieu devint une cour des miracles, **une sorte d'endroit où la société tolérait des actes qui sortaient du cadre. Cette situation fut reconnue par les artistes, les musiciens, les cinéastes, les hommes de musée..., à l'étranger aussi bien qu'en Suède.**

Mais, à mon avis, cette situation ne dura que de 1960 à 1968. En 1968, à la faveur des événements de mai, elle ne put plus durer, car elle aurait prouvé que le musée d'art moderne n'était simplement qu'une cour des miracles, un lieu clos, isolé, où tout était finalement permis puisque sans répercussion sur la réalité sociale.

On venait de réaliser que les événements de la rue avaient une force créatrice et destructive plus percutante. Ainsi, il nous faut prouver que les actions et les objets dans nos intuitions peuvent donner des exemples pour l'ensemble des activités renouvelant la mentalité des hommes. Il faut faire comprendre que nos manifestations, à leur échelon et avec leurs propres moyens d'existence, ont valeur de réalité et ainsi peuvent inspirer une nouvelle conception de la vie.

Opus : **Dans cette perspective, sur quels éléments porte votre analyse ?**

On pourrait sans doute en distinguer quatre : l'art contemporain, le musée proprement dit, le public et la notion de culture d'une société.

P. H. : **Nous sommes partis du dernier point et avons essayé de voir quel rôle le musée peut avoir au sein même de la cité. La mentalité qui régna pendant les journées de mai 1968 fut un état d'esprit fondé sur la spontanéité. Notre objectif est de faire en sorte que les idées qui élargissent la conception de la vie trouvent un endroit où elles peuvent s'exprimer et se développer de façon permanente.**

Nous nous sommes demandés s'il était possible de garder l'essentiel de la situation fondamentale de mai 1968, la « situation de la rue », où tout le monde, sans distinction classe, sans « attitude cultivé particulière, était là, sans se s rejeté.

A partir de cette question, r avons construit un modèle théor du musée moderne. Nous av imaginé un modèle abstrait à dimensions, d'allure sphérique. C sphère comprend quatre cou concentriques :

La couche ultérieure, l'envelc sphérique, qui discerne l'univers la vie quotidienne, se caracté par une concentration accél d'informations. Ces informat doivent être aussi peu rédigées possible. Ce sont pour nous matériaux bruts et directs. Là trouveront par exemple des scripteurs de toutes les ager

Cela représentera une sorte « degré zéro » de l'information lieu où l'individu est agressé toutes espèces d'informations sera évidemment impossible tenir des informations non n pulées, mais le fait même que informations seront souvent co dictoires créera une situation conflit, une situation critique situation de la rue est recré intensifiée, les conditions de cussion améliorées.

La deuxième couche sera rése aux ateliers, c'est-à-dire comp dra des espaces et des outils : locaux où l'on met à dispos des moyens de production, du marteau aux simples clous, pinceaux à l'ordinateur. Les sont fournis, mais rien n'est dé quant à leur usage, ni sur champs à exploiter, ni sur les des expériences. Le personne musée pourra agir comme ins

Modèle des activités futures du Mo Museet, en trois dimensions.

1. **Information primaire (communi téléprintée).**
2. **De l'espace et des outils po traitement des informations (des a pour le public, les artistes et le p nel du musée).**
3. **Information traitée (expositions films, musique, danse, théâtre...).**
4. **Collection d'art, archives de f Information traitée et gardée : mé**

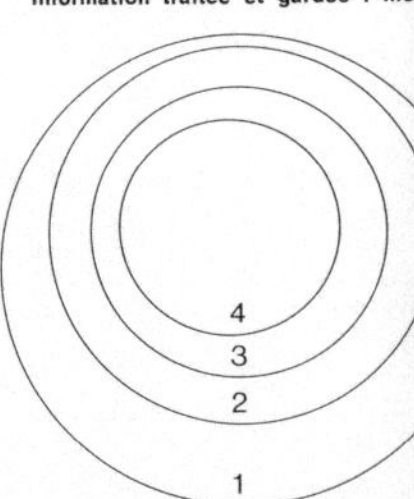

teur de ces machines. Ces a de travail pourront être emp soit par un artiste, soit pa groupe d'artistes, soit par nou par tout le monde. Les spéci dans les domaines de l'art

OPUS: We have so far spoken little of the artist and of contemporary art. Do they contribute to the changes in the conception of the museum?

P.H.: Yes, without a doubt. The evolution from 1960 to 1968 which I have briefly outlined is related to the conversation that has been established between artists and the museum. Driven by the demands of producing their art, artists were always pushing back against the confined limits of the enclosed space, against the institutional sclerosis of traditional museums. The Pop Art phenomenon involved reviving the connection with everyday life and, by its impact on day-to-day life, it tested in its own way the reality of the everyday. So the museum too had to rediscover these links.

The history of the modern art museum may very well be the history of "reconnections" that have not yet come to fruition.

OPUS: In this regard, it seems to me that artistic production since the beginning of the century, followed by contemporary productions, have been characterized by a reflexive approach to the history of art and the history of societies. Thus, there is an attempt these days to equate activities that are cultural in nature – art history, for example – with research activities of a scientific nature. Is this of interest to you?

P.H.: Very much so. We have to be continually available to receive and tap the constantly shifting information of our environment. The theoretical framework proposed earlier, which situates the role of the museum in society, in relation to the artists and the public, not only permits ongoing research activity concerning the systems of critical analysis capable of continuously processing information, but in fact it cannot function without it.

Conversations and discussions are the mainstay of our preoccupations in trying to channel and unpack information and its modes of presentation.

We would like to do what the Surrealists called a "critique of life". Of course, such a mechanism is of interest only if it both operates continuously and is grounded in a methodology. A genuine information science is being developed in conjunction with the new direction taken in the fields of science and humanities – computer science, cybernetics, linguistics, semiology, art history and

Moderna Museet / musée d'art moderne de Stockholm / ancien centre d'entraînement de base navale/sur île de Skeppsholm/conçu par Fredrik Blom en 1854/bâtiments reconstruits et agrandis/1958, devient musée d'art moderne / projet mené à bien par le conservateur Otte Sköld / reconstruction par l'architecte Per-Olof Olsson / inauguré le 9 mai 1958 / Salles d'exposition, salle de conférence et salle de projection, librairie, restaurant / à l'est, sculptures dans jardin, parmi arbres et fleurs/à l'entrée, les "quatre éléments" mobile de Calder/Collection : 2500 peintures et sculptures dont 1000 depuis 1958 ; moyenne de 100 par an / Budget : 320.000 couronnes par an, dont 165.000 pour l'art suédois/en 1964. A la faveur de l'exposition "le musée de nos désirs", reçu du gouvernement un crédit de 5.000.000 de Fr. (5 millions de nouveaux francs) / Les acquisitions se font aussi par dons privés (1994, Rolf de Maré) et par legs des "amis du Moderna Museet"/cette association fondée en 1953 compte 2800 membres dont 1200 âgés de moins de trente ans/organise visites commentées et voyages en Suède et étranger (U.S.A., U.R.S.S., Italie...) Autre association : le ciné-club ; pour adultes (créé en 1959, 6000 adhérents), pour enfants (créé en 1959, 5 à 8888 enfants)/ouvert tous les jours de 12h. à 22h./

l'aménagement de locaux différenciés selon les diverses fonctions que vous attribuez au « musée du futur » ?

P. H. : En principe, dans le bâtiment que nous faisons construire, nous n'avons pas pensé l'établissement de cloisons permanentes entre les endroits susceptibles de devenir un atelier de travail soit pour les artistes, le public ou nous-mêmes. Cela permet ainsi une libre communication à tous les niveaux, et facilite les échanges des idées à tout instant. Mais s'il arrive qu'une personne travaille sur un long projet, il sera certainement possible de l'isoler. Cette solution est d'ailleurs plus pratique en ce qui concerne la surveillance du musée.

Opus : Le gardiennage du musée est un problème épineux ; vous l'avez résolu de façon originale ?

P. H. : Au terme de gardien, nous préférons celui de moniteur, c'est-à-dire une personne qui non seulement « surveille » les outils, mais encore informe le public. Ce qu'il faut éviter, c'est évidemment la position policière, répressive, de la personne qui surveille. Au Moderna Museet, ce personnel est strictement féminin ; ce sont des « hôtesses », bien que je n'aime pas ce mot. De par leur rôle qui est essentiellement celui de renseigner et d'instruire le public, ces nouveaux « gardiens » détiennent des responsabilités vis-à-vis du public et participent ainsi à la vie du musée.

Opus : « L'éducation » du public semble un des obstacles majeurs qui pourrait ruiner l'utilité du musée d'art contemporain. Ce musée doit-il tenir compte de la population sans distinction de classes, ou, alors, doit-il continuer à s'adresser à un public de choix, une élite ? Comment parvenir à intéresser le plus grand nombre de gens possible ?

P. H. : A mon avis, ceci est un faux problème si l'on demande au seul musée une solution à cette question des plus importantes. Je puis répondre par deux constatations : lorsqu'un ouvrier vient réparer le toit ou la tuyauterie, c'est-à-dire qu'il entre au musée pour une cause professionnelle, il est le plus souvent intéressé (sur son temps payé bien sûr). Mais l'idée de pénétrer de sa propre initiative en tant que loisir ne lui vient certainement pas à l'esprit. Chaque classe possède une « attitude culturelle » et une « pratique cultivée » très fortement liées aux conventions et à l'éthos de chaque classe. Cette structure culturelle ne sera pas changée avant que la société de classe ait été brisée. Dans l'état actuel des choses, au mieux, nous ne pouvons qu'espérer contribuer à ce changement. Il faut avoir confiance dans l'activité artistique comme étant le moyen d'expression le plus subtil et en même temps le plus incisif.

Opus : Dans ce cas, la solution peut être purement politique ?

P. H. : Je ne crois pas que ce soit purement politique dans la mesure où l'ouvrier conservera la même attitude culturelle dictée par la morale de sa classe d'appartenance, même s'il accède à l'auto-gestion de son entreprise.

Opus : Oui, mais tout est lié ; je veux dire que la pensée politique, l'économique, les attitudes sociales, la production plastique forment un tout cohérent dans l'histoire de la société. Par exemple, le marché de l'art assigne à l'œuvre d'art, à la fonction du musée, des rapports faussés en leur affichant une image de marque précise : un objet de spéculation et un temple du savoir universel voué au culte de l'objet de « valeur »...

P. H. : En ce sens c'est politique. Mais je voudrais ajouter que depuis 1960 environ, le musée d'art moderne n'est plus compris comme un temple de la culture avec un grand « C ». Cette idée me semble périmée. La difficulté réside dans le fait qu'il faille faire connaître le musée d'art moderne comme une enclave libre, la seule peut-être qui puisse exister parmi les institutions. Cette obtention, cette exigence ne peuvent se faire qu'à partir d'un changement profond des structures globales de notre société, vers une prétendue civilisation des loisirs.

Opus : Et les galeries ? Et le marché de l'art ? Comment le Moderna Museet s'insère-t-il dans ce marché ?

P. H. : Notre mode de société étant ce qu'il est, on ne peut pas demander à l'artiste d'être un mendiant. Les galeries sont utiles, mais il me semble que depuis 1960, la commercialisation de l'art est poussée à l'extrême. Les galeries sont allées trop loin et cela est très dangereux. Les marchands et les artistes ont été corrompus par la facilité de cette « société de consommation » qui ne considère l'objet d'art que comme un produit de spéculation. Il nous est bien sûr impossible d'arrêter un tel système. En fait, nous avons essayé d'agir de telle sorte que l'on n'achète pas dans les galeries, mais qu'on achète directement aux artistes ; ceux-ci viennent proposer leurs œuvres en déposant au musée soit l'œuvre même, soit des dispositives. Notre musée devient ainsi une sorte de place libre où artiste et public se rencontrent dans des conditions plus saines. Cette tâche supplémentaire, nécessaire à mon avis, crée une situation nouvelle, parallèle et complémentaire qui permet d'échapper un peu à un système de cotation faussée qui ne correspond en rien à la réalité des faits plastiques.

Opus : Jusqu'à présent, on a peu parlé de l'artiste et de l'art contemporain. Contribuèrent-ils aux changements dans la conception du musée ?

P. H. : Sans aucun doute. Toute l'évolution de 1960 à 1968 que j'ai [illegible] logue qui s'est instauré entre l'artiste et le musée. L'artiste, poussé par les exigences de la production de son art, faisait reculer sans cesse les limites exiguës de ce lieu clos, de cette institution sclérosée qu'était le musée traditionnel. Le phénomène du Pop'Art est une production qui renoue le lien avec la vie de tous les jours, qui par son impact sur le quotidien, éprouve à sa manière la réalité de ce quotidien. Il fallait donc que le musée retrouve lui aussi ces contacts.

L'histoire du musée d'art moderne, ce serait peut-être l'histoire de ces « retrouvailles » qui n'ont pas encore abouti.

Opus : A ce propos, il me semble que la production artistique depuis le début du siècle, puis les productions contemporaines, se caractérisent par une démarche réflexive sur l'histoire de l'art, l'histoire des sociétés. A ce titre, actuellement, on tente d'assimiler les activités dites culturelles, l'histoire de l'art par exemple, à des activités de recherche de type scientifique. Cela vous concerne-t-il ?

P. H. : Très directement. Nous devons être disponibles continuellement pour recevoir et capter les informations sans cesse mouvantes de notre environnement. Le schéma théorique proposé précédemment, qui situe le rôle du musée dans la société, par rapport aux artistes et au public, non seulement permet, mais encore ne peut fonctionner que sur une activité perpétuelle de recherche concernant les systèmes d'analyse critique capables de traiter en permanence les informations.

Dialogues et débats sont le lot de nos préoccupations pour essayer de canaliser, de dépouiller l'information, ses modes de présentation.

Nous voudrions faire ce que les « Surréalistes » appelaient « la critique de la vie ». Un tel mécanisme n'a bien sûr d'intérêt que s'il fonctionne en permanence et que s'il se fonde sur une méthodologie. Une véritable science de l'information est en train de s'élaborer corrélativement à la nouvelle orientation prise par les sciences et sciences humaines : informatique, cybernétique, linguistique, sémiologie, histoire de l'art... remise en cause des concepts de théorie, d'histoire, d'espace, de temps, de signe...

Voilà, à mon avis, quelques indications qui définiront les options fondamentales du musée d'art contemporain.

Opus : Quel est alors le rôle du conservateur ?

P. H. : Le « musée du futur » sera donc considéré comme une base permettant des contacts directs entre artiste, public et société. Il sera le lieu par excellence de la communication, de la rencontre, de la diffusion ; il sera un instrument de réflexion, un centre de recherche para-scientifique sur les pratiques socio-culturelles présentes et à venir.

Le conservateur sera un coordinateur de ce centre de recherche.

Enquête de Yann PAVIE

Moderna Museet :
1 Happening « Zebra », 1969
2 Happening « Bombay Free School », 1968

62 63

Principales expositions

1958 : *Le Corbusier* - 1959 : *Matta* - 1960 : *Jacques Villon, Sam Francis* - 1961 : *Paul Klee, Art cinétique, « Le stedelijk museum »* - 1962 : *Quatre Américains (Johns, Leslie, Rauschenberg, Stankiewiecz), Arp* - 1963 : *Ben Shahn, Pollock, August Strindberg, Fautrier* - 1964 : *le Pop Art américain, « Art et béton », Léger, Hundertwasser* - 1965 : *Bacon, Rauschenberg, Kandinsky, Rosenquist, Van Gogh, « le monde intérieur et le monde extérieur »* - 1966 : *Exposition Dada, Appel, « Elle, cathédrale construite par Niki de Saint-Phalle, Tinguely et Per Olof Ultveld », Oldenburg, la collection Peggy Guggenheim* - 1967 : *Nolde, « terre, ciel, enfer ; trois Danois : Henry Heerup, Palle Nielsen, C.-H. Pedersen », Wilfredo Lam, Meret Oppenheim, Fontana, John Hearthfield, Magritte, Hausmann* - 1968 : *Warhol, « le langage de la révolution », Saul Steinberg, « la collection Gérard Bonnier », Tatlin, « Le modèle », J.-P. Raynaud, Eva Aeppli, Wialdyslaw Hassor* - 1969 : *Le Parc, Les Ballets Suédois, Alvar Aalto, Raimund Abraham : « Zip Zones » et Friedrich St Florian : « Imaginary Architecture », Ernst, « La poésie doit être faite par tous - transformer le monde »* - 1970 : *Kienholz, Surréalisme, « Alternative Suédoise », Piotr Kowalski.*

En plus des expositions rassemblant les œuvres d'un artiste, d'une « école », où, selon un thème particulier, le Moderna Museet présente des manifestations annexes et organise des expositions à l'étranger, soit seul, pour l'art international (1970 : « Tatlin » à Munich et Venise (Biennale), soit avec la collaboration du comité Nunsku pour l'art suédois (1970 : « Alternative suédoise » à l'A.R.C.).

Quant aux manifestations annexes qui « occasionnent de violentes critiques dans la presse suédoise et étrangère », elles concernent soit des concerts de musique contemporaine, soit des expositions d'architecture ou de photographie, soit des soirées (conférences, happenings...) en corrélation avec les principales expositions :

1962 : « John Cage et le Zen », présentation de « Où allons-nous » et de « Que faisons-nous ».

1963 : « Poésie de la scène » avec J.-C. Lambert et J.-L. Philippe.

1964 : « Cinq soirées new-yorkaises » avec Merce Cunningham et la Dance Company, J. Cage, David Tudor, Rauschenberg, et Fahlström, Yvonne Rainer et Robert Morris.

1966 : « Soirées Dada », « Jerzy Grotowski », première représentation à l'étranger du fameux théâtre-laboratoire polonais. « Massage », happening de Claes Oldenburg.

1967 : « Kunst und Politik », conférence de John Heartfield.

1969 : « Zebra », pantomine et musique.

1970 : « La télévision du peuple ».

Les principales acquisitions du Moderna Museet

1958 : *Archipenko*, Collage avec gouache.
1959 : *Brauner*, La découverte de la conscience.
Ernst, L'été imaginaire *(1927)*.
Matta, L'ouverture de l'être.
1960 : *M. Duchamp*, Roto-reliefs.
H. Michaux, Composition.
Soto, Vibration *(un cinétique chez les « Surréalistes » !)*.
1961 : *M. Duchamp*, La mariée mise à nue par ses célibataires, même.
Fontana, Concept spatial *(1959)*.
Sam Francis, Au-delà du jaune *(1958-60)*.
Mondrian, Composition avec un rectangle bleu *(1938)*.
Tapies, Composition avec une zone grise *(1960)*.
1962 : *Kurt Schwitters*, Avec l'araignée, *collage (1921)* ; Composition, *collage (1936)* ; Horizontal, *collage (1947)*.
Arp, Boule nuageuse.
et... M. Duchamp, Boîte en valise.
1963 : *Jasper Johns*, Slow field *(1962) et encore un Duchamp*, Objet dard *(1961)*.
1964 : *Jim Dine*, Outils noirs dans un paysage *(1962)*.
Picabia, Prenez garde à la peinture *(1916)*.
Rosenquist, Je vous aime avec ma Ford *(1961)*.
Segal, Homme à bicyclette *(1961)*.
Oldenburg, Table de ping-pong *(1964)*.
Niki de Saint-Phalle, Composition *(1956)* ; L'accouchement rose *(1964)*.
Spoerri, Collection d'épices *(1963)*.
1965 : *Kandinsky*, Aquarelle n° 6 *(1916)*.
Tinguely, Meta-Matic n° 17 *(1959)*
et toujours Duchamp, Ready-mades divers... ; Stoppages-Etalon *(1913-1914)* ; Porte-bouteilles *(1914)* ; Lepeigne *(1916)* ; Un bruit secret *(1916)* ; Fontaine *(1917)* ; Pliant de voyage *(1917)* ; Air de Paris *(1919)* ; Pourquoi ne pas éternuer *(1921)*.
1966 : *(Donation Rolf de Maré) à l'exception de deux œuvres de Man Ray, elle concerne essentiellement l'art français du début du siècle :*
Braque, Le compotier *(1908)* ; La Roche-Guyon : le château *(1909)* ; Nature morte au violon *(1911)* ; Trois barques : ciel nuageux *(1929)*.
(Derain, Marie Laurencin, G. Rouault.)
Picasso, Fernande *(1910)*.
Léger, Le pont du bateau *(1919)* ; Les deux grâces *(1929)* ; Les danseuses aux clefs *(1930)*.
Le Corbusier, Nature morte *(1922)*.
(Fautrier, Man Ray.)
1967 : Crédit de cinq millions de N.F.
Les achats, cette année-là, sont fort nombreux et recouvrent à peu près toutes les grandes orientations prises par l'art contemporain depuis le début du siècle : Albers, Bacon, Balla, Calder, De Chirico, Dali, Dubuffet, Ernst, Giacometti, Gonzalez, Kandinsky, Kirchner, Klein, Lam, Laurens, Magritte, Matta, Miro, Mondrian, Moore, Nolde, Oldenburg, Oppenheim, Picabia, Picasso, Pollock, Rauschenberg, Raymond Duchamp, Villon, Siqueiros, Tinguely.
1968 : *Allen Jones*, Femme entrevue *(1965)*.
Matisse, Apollon *(1953)*.
M. Raysse, France verte *(1964)*.
César, Expansion contrôlée rose *(1968)*.
1969 : *Ozenfant, Picabia, Moholy-Nagy ; année suédoise : Billgren*, Le corridor *(1969)*.
John-e Franzen : Hell's Angels. United States of America *(1966)*.
Olle Kaks, Vie *(1969)* ; Terre *(1969)*.
Eva Aeppli, La table.

BIBLIOGRAPHIE

P. Bourdieu et A. Darbel : L'amour de l'art *(Ed. de Minuit, 1966)*.
P. Gaudibert : « Musée d'Art Moderne, animation et contestation », revue d'esthétique.
J.-C. Lebenzteyn : « L'espace de l'art », Critique *(n° 275, avril 1970)*.

64

Exposition « Le Modèle », 1968

so on – challenging concepts of theory, history, space, time, the sign …

These are, in my opinion, some indications that will define the fundamental options of the contemporary art museum.

OPUS: What then is the role of the curator?

P.H.: The "museum of the future" will be regarded as a base for direct contacts between artists, the public and society. It will be the locus par excellence of communication, meeting and dissemination. It will be an instrument of reflection, a center of para-scientific research into present-day and future socio-cultural practices.

The curator will be a coordinator in this center of research.

Interview from the magazine *Opus International*, nos. 24–25, 1971.

Exhibitions at Moderna Museet 1966–1973:

1966
Moderna Museet Visits Lund, 15 January–20 February
Dada Exhibition, 3 February–27 March
Karel Appel. Paintings 1947–1965, 26 February–27 March
Africans Weave, 5–27 March
Hello Town, 2–24 April
Louis Isadore Kahn. Architect, 19–30 April
The Era of the Artist. An Epoch in the History of Swedish Photography, 1–30 June (at Stockholm City Museum)
She – A Cathedral by Niki de Saint Phalle, Jean Tinguely, P. O. Ultvedt, 4 June–4 September
The Hulton Collection, 9 July–6 August
Anna Stridh in Torpa, 13 August–4 September
Claes Oldenburg. Sculptures and Drawings, 17 September–30 October
Young Photographers 1966, 8–30 October
Moderna Museet Visits Skövde, 2–23 October
Young People from Egypt Weave 1961–1966, 3–20 November
Moderna Museet Visits Oslo, 12 November–11 December
Peggy Guggenheim Collection, Venice, 26 November–8 January, 1967

1967
News Shots – Press Photographers from Four Evening Papers Reflect the Present Day Life, January
Emil Nolde 1867–1956. Paintings and Prints, 14 January–15 February
Henry Heerup, Carl-Henning Pedersen, Palle Nielsen. Earth Heaven Hell, 25 February–2 April
Wifredo Lam. The Heart's Thickets, Weapons and Fruits, 8 April–7 May
Meret Oppenheim, 15 April–28 May
Olle Bonniér. Minos's Palace. Communications – Simultaneously Insulated in Man and Open Towards Cosmos, 29 April–4 June
Édouard Boubat. Moments in Life, 12 May–4 June
The S. Grace and Philip Sandblom Collection, 9 June–16 July
Lucio Fontana. Ideas on Space, 26 August–1 October
John Heartfield. Photo Montage Artist, 1 September–1 October
Plastic, 22–24 September
Young Photographers 67, 28 September–17 October
René Magritte. Retrospective, 7 October–12 November
Raoul Hausmann, 21 October–19 November
Us in Pictures, 10 November–December
Shalom Moskowitz from Safed. From the Biblical World, 15 November–17 December
Bror Hjorth, 1 December–21 January, 1968

1968

Moderna Museet Visits Tammerfors, 9 February–10 March
Andy Warhol, 10 February–17 March
The Language of the Revolution. Communist Posters from Across the Globe, 23 March–5 May
Saul Steinberg. Drawings and Collages 1955–1967, 7 April–12 May
Walter Hirsch. London, 13 April 1968, 9 am to 11 pm, 22 May–5 June
From the Gerard Bonnier Collection, 6 June–25 August
Vladimir Tatlin, 3 July–1 October
The Model. A Model for a Qualitative Society, 30 September–23 October
The Olympic Games in Pictures, 1 October–30 November
Eva Aeppli, 5 October–3 November
Jean Pierre Raynaud, 5 October–3 November
Władysław Hasior, 9 November–15 December

1969

Lucien Clergue. Photographs 1954–1967, 8 January–16 February
Julio Le Parc. Experimental Place to Experience the Movement of the Eye, Body and Objects, 11 January–16 February
Remo Bianco. Chemical Art. Sephadex – An Aesthetic Experiment, 25 January–16 February
The Swedish Ballet in Paris 1920–1925, 27 February–7 April
Alvar Aalto, 18 April–1 June
Raimund Abraham and Friedrich St. Florian. Imaginary Architecture, 11 May–21 June
Young Photographers 69, 22 May–30 June
Sculpture for the Blind and the Seeing, 12 June–31 August
Max Ernst. Paintings, Collages, Frottages, Drawings, Prints, Books, Sculptures 1917–1969, 13 September–2 November
Seppo Saves, 27 September–19 October
Sven Erixson, 8 November–4 January, 1970
Poetry Must Be Made by All! Transform the World! 15 November–18 January, 1970

1970

Edward Kienholz. 11+11 Tableaux, 17 January–1 March
Surrealism?, 7 March–12 April
David Octavius Hill & Robert Adamson. Two Camera Classics, 29 March–29 April
Anders Petersen. A Reeperbahn Neighbourhood, 9–31 May
Alternative Suédoise/Swedish Alternative, 24 October–29 November
Oscar Gustave Rejlander. A Swedish Photographer in Victorian Britain, 29 October–29 November
Posters from Italy and Berkeley, USA, 30 October–10 January, 1971

Martin Holmgren. Shapes Looking for a Common Centre. Sculptures and Drawings 1948–1969, 7 November–13 December
Bernhard and Hilla Becher. Form Through Function, 14 November–13 December
Piotr Kowalski, 5 December–6 January, 1971

1971
Günther Uecker. Visual Objects 1957–1970, 16 January–28 February
Joseph Beuys. Actions/Aktionen, 16 January–28 February
Series, 20 January–14 February
Björn Lövin. The Infinite Consumer and "Mr P's Monies", 20 February–11 April
Report from Hallsta, 1–28 March
Richard Paul Lohse, 13 March–18 April
Moderna Museet Visits Liljevalchs, 19 May–5 September
Odd Uhrbom. My Home is Palestine, 21 May–24 June
Utopias and Visions 1871–1981, 9 June–29 August
Gun Kessle (Images) and Jan Myrdal (Text). The People and the Walls of Power, 2 July–29 August
André Kertész. Photographs 1913–1971, 4 September–10 October
Posters from Cuba, 11 September–17 October
Jacques de la Villeglé. Retrospective 1949–1971, 16 October–21 November
Paul Thek. Pyramid, 6 November–9 January, 1972
Vlassis Caniaris. Greek Testimony, 27 November–16 January, 1972

1972
Gifts from the Friends of Moderna Museet, 22 January–13 February
Pictures from the 1910s. Paintings, Drawings, Sculptures, Posters, Films, Photos, Newspaper Illustrations and Texts That Make Us See and Experience, 5 February–9 April
George Grosz. Watercolours and Drawings, 19 February–19 March
Douglass Kneedler. Pigs – svin, 25 March–30 April
People's Pictures, 3 April–16 May
Albin Amelin. Retrospective, 22 April–28 May
Ove Holmquist and Anders Petersen. Immigrants, 27 April–7 May
Eustachy Kossakowski. 6 Metres in Front of Paris. 159 Photographs, 29 April–8 May
Carsten Regild. Necropolis, 6 May–11 June
Save Our Environment, 3 June–27 August
Carl Fredrik Reutersvärd. Kilroy, 3 June–3 September
Jacob Riis. How the Other Half Lived, 30 September–5 November
Jean Tinguely 1954–1972, 7 October–3 December
Åke Karlung. Aliena Kadabra – A Porno-Puritanical Failure, 29 November–28 January, 1973
Ernst Ludwig Kirchner 1880–1938. Watercolours and Drawings from the Franz Josef Kohl-Weigand Collection, 16 December–21 January, 1973

1973

KRO Lottery. The Swedish Artists' National Organisation, 10–25 February

Visible and Invisible. The New Images of Science, 17 March–13 May

Enrico Baj. The Funeral of the Anarchist Pinelli. A Painting, 12 May–17 June

Lima, 18 May–2 September

Out of Our Heads. Pictures from LP Sleeves, 19 May–2 September

Louise Nevelson 1955–1972, 8 September–14 October

Young Americans. Drawings and Prints, 15 September–21 October

New York Collection for Stockholm, 27 October–9 December

The River and the Forest, 3 November–9 December

Salvador Dalí, 26 December–24 February, 1974

Index of Names:

Images:

Abbreviations
MMA The Moderna Museet archives
MA The Moderna Museet public archive (Myndighetsarkivet)
PHA The Pontus Hultén archive

p. 1: Magnus Wibom. MMA MA Ö7a:1
pp. 2–3: Hans Hammarskiöld. MMA
pp. 4–5: Hans Hammarskiöld. MMA
pp. 6–7: Nils-Göran Hökby. MMA
pp. 8–9: Erik Cornelius. MMA MA Ö7a:2
pp. 10–11: Ad Petersen. MMA PHA 4.2.58
pp. 12–13: Hickey & Robertson. MMA PHA 4.2.58
pp. 14–15: Erik Cornelius. MMA MA Ö7a:5
p. 16: Benno Movin-Hermes. The Moderna Museet Collection, FM 1974 020 081. Repro photo: Albin Dahlström/Moderna Museet
pp. 22, 26–27: Åsa Lundén/ Moderna Museet
pp. 30–31: Erik Cornelius. MMA MA Ö7a:2
p. 34: Albin Dahlström/Moderna Museet. MMA MA B5:2
p. 37: Nils-Göran Hökby. MMA (above). Nils-Göran Hökby. MMA MA Ö7a:2 (below)
p. 38: Tobias Fischer/Moderna Museet. The Moderna Museet Collection, FM 1968 004 001, FM 1968 004 002
p. 41: Nils-Göran Hökby. MMA
p. 43: Erik Cornelius. MMA
p. 44: Okänd fotograf. MMA
p. 46: Erik Cornelius. MMA MA Ö7a:4
p. 49: Erik Cornelius. MMA MA Ö7a:5
p. 62: Hans Hammarskiöld. MMA
p. 65: Albin Dahlström/Moderna Museet. The Moderna Museet Collection, MOM/2005/935
p. 66: Magnus Wibom. MMA MA Ö7a:1
p. 69: Hans Hammarskiöld. MMA (above). Magnus Wibom. MMA MA Ö7a:1 (below)
pp. 72–73: Albin Dahlström/Moderna Museet. The Moderna Museet Collection, MOM/2005/716
p. 77: Albin Dahlström/Moderna Museet. F1a:32
p. 78: Hans Hammarskiöld. MMA
p. 81: Hans Hammarskiöld. MMA
p. 92: Ad Petersen. MMA PHA 4.2.58
p. 95: Albin Dahlström/Moderna Museet. MMA PHA 4.2.56
pp. 98–99: James Mathews/The Museum of Modern Art. MMA PHA 4.2.58
p. 102: Albin Dahlström/Moderna Museet. MMA PHA 4.2.55
p. 105: Ad Petersen. MMA PHA 4.2.58 (above). James Mathews/The Museum of Modern Art. MMA PHA 4.2.58 (below)
p. 108: James Mathews/The Museum of Modern Art. MMA PHA 4.2.58
pp. 120, 123, 126, 129, 130, 133, 134, 137: Albin Dahlström/Moderna Museet. Pontus Hultén's Collection of Books, Moderna Museet
p. 148: Unknown photographer. MMA PHA 4.2.40
p. 151: Albin Dahlström/Moderna Museet. MMA PHA 4.3.3
p. 154: Albin Dahlström/Moderna Museet. MMA PHA 4.3.1
p. 159: Albin Dahlström/Moderna Museet. MMA PHA 4.3.1
pp. 168, 173, 176–177, 179: Albin Dahlström/Moderna Museet

Pontus Hultén and Moderna Museet. From Stockholm to Paris

Editor: Anna Tellgren
Managing editor: Teresa Hahr
Translations: Gabriella Berggren from Swedish, Gila Walker from French
Proofreader: Tas Skorupa
Pre-press: Albin Dahlström
Graphic design: Karl Stefan Andersson
Printed by: By Wind, 2023

The text on pp. 169–180 from *Opus International*, nos. 24–25, 1971, is reprinted with permission from the author, Yann Pavie.

Photo credits: Erik Cornelius; Hans Hammarskiöld Heritage; Hickey & Robertson/Courtesy of Menil Archives, The Menil Collection, Houston; Nils-Göran Hökby; Benno Movin-Hermes; Digital image, The Museum of Modern Art, New York/Scala, Florence; Magnus Wibom

ISBN 978-91-984573-4-6 (Moderna Museet)
ISBN 978-3-7533-0396-3 (Verlag der Buchhandlung Walther und Franz König)

www.modernamuseet.se
www.buchhandlung-walther-koenig.de

Published by Moderna Museet and Verlag der Buchhandlung Walther und Franz König, Cologne
Printed in Sweden

Distribution:
Buchhandlung Walther König, Ehrenstr. 4, D-50672 Cologne
+49 (0) 221 20 59 6 53, verlag@buchhandlung-walther-koenig.de

Cover: From *She – A Cathedral Constructed by Niki de Saint Phalle, Jean Tinguely, Per Olof Ultvedt*, ed. Pontus Hultén, Moderna Museet exhibition catalogue no. 54, Stockholm: Moderna Museet, 1966.